*Paratextual Communities*

*Paratextual Communities*

# American Avant-Garde Poetry since 1950

Susan
Vanderborg

Southern Illinois University Press
*Carbondale and Edwardsville*

Library of Congress Cataloging-in-Publication Data

Vanderborg, Susan, 1967–
    Paratextual communities : American avant-garde poetry since 1950 / Susan
Vanderborg.
        p. cm.
    Includes bibliographical references (p. ) and index.
        1. American poetry—20th century—History and criticism.  2. Avant-garde
(Aesthetics)—United States—History—20th century.  3. Experimental poetry, American—
History and criticism.  4. Poetry—History and criticism—Theory, etc.  5. Intertextuality.
I. Title.

PS323.5 .V34 2001
811'.540911—dc21
ISBN 0-8093-2323-0 (alk. paper)                    00-052219

The paper used in this publication meets the minimum requirements of American National
Standard for Information Sciences—Permanence of Paper for Printed Library Materials,
ANSI Z39.48-1992. ♾

To Hannah and Alex with love

# Contents

# Figures

# Acknowledgments

$I$ wish to express my warmest gratitude to Marjorie Perloff for her detailed and incisive commentary on drafts of this book. The thoughtful responses of Albert Gelpi, Shirley Heath, Priscilla Wald, and Ming-Qian Ma have also been invaluable in reviewing the chapter arguments. I would like to thank Charles Bernstein, Lorenzo Thomas, Johanna Drucker, and Susan Howe for their kind responses to inquiries about textual editions.

Grants from the University of South Carolina's College of Liberal Arts and the Office of Sponsored Programs and Research were instrumental in enabling me to conduct research for this project and to bring it to completion.

I wish to thank Kathleen Kageff and Karl Kageff, my editors at Southern Illinois University Press, for their painstaking work on the book. Thanks also to my research assistants Patricia Stubblefield, Brad O'Brien, and Dollie Newhouse for their dedicated help in preparing the manuscript.

Lastly, I am deeply indebted to my family for their faith and patient support during all the stages of the writing.

A previous version of chapter 2 was published as "'Who Can Say Who Are Citizens?': Causal Mythology in Charles Olson's Polis," in *Modern Language Quarterly* 59.3 (Sept. 1998): 363–84.

A previous version of a portion of chapter 3 was published as "'Because These Letters Are Unnecessary': Translation and Community in Jack Spicer's *After Lorca*," in *The Recovery of the Public World: Essays on Poetics in Honour of Robin Blaser*, ed. Charles Watts and Edward Byrne (Burnaby, British Columbia: Talonbooks, 1999): 169–77.

A previous version of chapter 4 was published as "The Communal Lyric: Palimpsest in the Corpus of Susan Howe." Copyright 1998 from *New Definitions of Lyric: Theory, Technology, and Culture,* ed. Mark Jeffreys (New York: Garland, 1998): 99–126. Reproduced by permission of Taylor & Francis, Inc./Routledge, Inc. http://www.routledge-ny.com.

Permission to quote from the following sources is gratefully acknowledged:

Susan Howe, *My Emily Dickinson*. Used by permission of North Atlantic Books.

Herman Melville, *Billy Budd, Sailor (An Inside Narrative): Reading Text and Genetic Text,* edited by Harrison Hayford and Merton M. Sealts Jr. Copyright 1962 by the University of Chicago Press and used by permission of the University of Chicago Press.

Jack Spicer, *The Collected Books of Jack Spicer.* Copyright 1975 by the Estate of Jack Spicer and used by permission of Black Sparrow Press.

Lorenzo Thomas, *Chances are Few.* Copyright 1979 by Lorenzo Thomas and used by permission of Blue Wind Press and Lorenzo Thomas.

Charles Olson, *The Collected Poems of Charles Olson,* ed. George F. Butterick, 1987; *The Maximus Poems,* ed. George F. Butterick, 1983; *Collected Prose,* ed. Donald Allen and Benjamin Friedlander, 1997 (Berkeley: University of California Press). Courtesy of University of California Press.

# Abbreviations

**Charles Bernstein**

*AP—A Poetics*
*CD—Content's Dream: Essays 1975–1984*
*DC—Dark City*
*II—Islets/Irritations*
*MW—My Way: Speeches and Poems*
*RR—Republics of Reality: 1975–1995*
*RT—Rough Trades*
*S—The Sophist*

**Johanna Drucker**

*FW—Figuring the Word: Essays on Books, Writing, and Visual Poetics*
*H—The History of the/my Wor(l)d*
*S—Simulant Portrait*
*VW—The Visible Word: Experimental Typography and Modern Art, 1909–1923*

**Susan Howe**

*B—The Birth-mark: Unsettling the Wilderness in American Literary History*
BI—Interview with Tom Beckett
FI—Interview with Janet Ruth Falon
*MED—My Emily Dickinson*
*NM—The Nonconformist's Memorial: Poems by Susan Howe*
*S—Singularities*

**Herman Melville**

*BB—Billy Budd, Sailor (An Inside Narrative): Reading Text and Genetic Text*

**Charles Olson**

*CP—The Collected Poems of Charles Olson, Excluding the* Maximus *Poems*
*CPr—Collected Prose*
*LO—Letters for* Origin *1950–1956*
*M—The Maximus Poems*
*ML—Mayan Letters*
*MU1—Muthologos: The Collected Lectures and Interviews, volume 1*

MU2—*Muthologos: The Collected Lectures and Interviews, volume 2*
PM—*Pleistocene Man: Letters from Charles Olson to John Clarke During October 1965*

**Jack Spicer**

CB—*The Collected Books of Jack Spicer*
L—*The House That Jack Built: The Collected Lectures of Jack Spicer*
O—*One Night Stand & Other Poems*

**Lorenzo Thomas**

B—*The Bathers*
C—*Chances are Few*

*Paratextual Communities*

# 1

## *Introduction*

Syntax, the garterbelt of language     Just a reptilian emphasis
Melodramatic *forms,* not *contents* – Not content with content     One
swears off to again     Palace starship coded dextrous thought crimes
(hidden from mikes) which monikers we are all one display     Your
name widens with rosy emphasis mistaken for a gift     Stilts
And something else on tight
                    —"Getting Ready To Have Been Frightened"

Altering textual roles might bring us closer to altering the larger
social roles of which textual ones are a feature. READING: not the
glazed gaze of the consumer, but the careful attention of a producer,
or co-producer. The transformer. (capacitators? resistors?) Full of
care. It's not a product that is produce, but a *production,* an event, a
praxis, a model for future practice.
                    —"Text and Context"

$B$oth of the above quotes are taken from compositions by Bruce
Andrews, an experimental poet and the cofounder of the New York poetics jour-
nal *L=A=N=G=U=A=G=E* (1978–1981). The first passage, from a late seven-
ties poem in his collection *Getting Ready To Have Been Frightened* (72),[1] demon-
strates the interpretive challenge posed by Andrews's "Melodramatic *forms.*" As
the pun on "content" suggests, the run-on word sequences, the sudden shifts from
abstractions to concrete images, and the lack of referential contexts all compli-
cate the project of finding clear signifieds for the words. The habit that is being
forsworn here is deliberately left ambiguous. The allusions to displays, mikes, and
fantasy settings of palaces or starships might be satirizing an infatuation with
Hollywood broadcasts whose "coded dextrous thought" encourages viewers to
be passive consumers. Or are we being invited to indulge in hidden "thought

crimes" against clichéd media formats? The difficulty with communication seems appropriate to the passage's portrayal of social exchanges as mistaken "emphas[es]" in which the simplest gesture of introduction ("Your / name") can become a stilted, perhaps clownish, performance. Even the standardized syntax that one takes for granted, his garterbelt metaphor implies, may be an outdated fashion, one of many possible arrangements of signifiers.

The second passage, an excerpt from a 1977 poetics essay reprinted in *The L=A=N=G=U=A=G=E Book* (36), asks us not to dismiss the poetry as esoteric word games but to consider the "larger social" strategy of linguistic disruptions that require greater audience participation in interrogating the codes by which language patterns construct meaning. Andrews's poetics statements underscore a compelling paradox in contemporary American experimental poetry. Many of the post–World War II avant-garde authors who have written most passionately and extensively about the nature of a public poetry and the politics of poetic form have also generated the most debate over the accessibility of their own texts. Critics ask how these writers can speak of a public or communal poetry when their texts disrupt signification so pervasively at the level of semantics, syntax, subject position, and punctuation.

When read side by side, Andrews's two textual styles offer a more complex picture of his poetics than either one alone. Both the essay and the poem are creative productions that play with double entendres, associative rhythm, and parenthetical qualification to foreground the grammatical and sound patterns that mediate meaning. He invites us to compare the two genres by having each incorporate visual elements of the other's form. The poetic page in "Getting Ready To Have Been Frightened," for instance, juxtaposes elliptical phrases at the top of the page with denser sections resembling prose poetry (see fig. 1.1), while the essay, like many Language prose texts, includes fragments lineated as poems (see fig. 1.2).

The difference between them is that the essay, even while calling attention to the artifice of its own composition, discusses the significance of Andrews's linguistic experiments more directly than the poetry does. Its accessibility is in part due to its own more regularized syntax, with sentences bracketing clearly connected fragments, but it is also a result of the argumentative details. The essay provides specific interpretive options for a signifier such as "reading" and suggests the implications of the different choices. In contrast to conventional exegesis, Andrews describes this process as a "counter-explanation," a "rebuff which shows a larger possibility—an emptied cipher that speaks of all the productions we can fill it with" ("Text and Context" 35), yet the essay still outlines some of the hoped-for outcomes of the redefinition of reading.

The repeated use of "we" in the essay is equally telling. Where the poem fea-

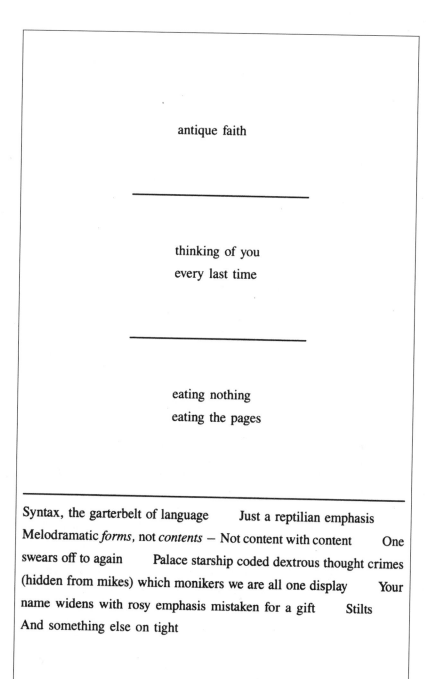

antique faith

_____

thinking of you
every last time

_____

eating nothing
eating the pages

_____

Syntax, the garterbelt of language     Just a reptilian emphasis
Melodramatic *forms,* not *contents* — Not content with content     One
swears off to again     Palace starship coded dextrous thought crimes
(hidden from mikes) which monikers we are all one display     Your
name widens with rosy emphasis mistaken for a gift     Stilts
And something else on tight

Fig. 1.1 Excerpt from Bruce Andrews, *Getting Ready To Have Been Frightened,* p. 72.
Copyright 1988 by Bruce Andrews. Reprinted by permission of Roof Books.

Binary, with the text as switchman.
Blurs, so fast = mesh

Texts read the reader.

◆§ Altering textual roles might bring us closer to altering the larger so-
cial roles of which textual ones are a feature. READING: not the glazed
gaze of the consumer, but the careful attention of a producer, or co-
producer. The transformer. (capacitators? resistors?) Full of care. It's not
a product that is produce, but a *production*, an event, a praxis, a model
for future practice. The domination of nature can find a critique here as
well—not in abstinence. Not aleatory.

From each according to
To each according to

A semantic atmosphere, or milieu, rather than the possessive individu-
alism of reference.

Indexicality.
Absolute.
Absolution.

Such work has a utopian force only begun to be revealed.

◆§ Language is an Other which imposed meanings attempt, luckily un-
successfully, to disguise for us. The 'Primal Lack'. Life against death. It
is not a monologic communication, but a spatial interaction fore-
grounded within a frame of our own generosity. Our gifts, its physical
integrity.
  Stay inside. It is all here. The non-imperial state: without need for
the expansion or externalization that comes from the refusal to re-
distribute the surplus at home. The same holds for a non-imperial or
language-centered writing.
  Surplus of signifier = the floating signifier. *Mana.* trace.
  Engulfment, flooding of signifiers without predetermined significa-
tion. Instead, the cliches of existentialism—freedom, surplus of signi-
fiers, *choice as constitutive* & we do it ourselves.
  Politics not concealed any longer.

Decontextualization.

Fig. 1.2 Excerpt from Bruce Andrews, "Text and Context," *The L=A=N=G=U=A=G=E
Book*, ed. Bruce Andrews and Charles Bernstein, Southern Illinois University Press, p.
36. © 1984 by Andrews and Bernstein, reprinted by permission.

tures decontextualized pronouns and links the infrequent "we" voice to an advertising display, the essay explores the metaphors of a "body politic" (37) and of linguistic investigations as "a creation of a community" (35), with the reader and writer negotiating a "charter or a town-meeting" (35). It ends by declaring, "Readers embody texts" (38), as if part of the "future practice" (36), the poet's call for readers to become coproducers rather than consumers of textual meaning, has already been accomplished.

What Andrews's reader discovers, in other words, is not a poetry supplemented by straightforward poetics statements but a dialogue between two interconnected literary genres that qualify each other's premises and complement each other's styles. This relation between Andrews's essays and poetry is part of a broader phenomenon. Since the fifties, many of the American avant-garde poets who theorize the public or communal nature of disjunctive poetries have created divided formats in their writing, in which extended discussions of community and audience take place in paratextual spaces set apart from the poetic text. By *paratext,* I refer specifically to the highly creative essays, notes, prefaces, and source documents that these authors provide with their experimental poetry.[2] Paratexts offer a forum in which the author can present ideological agendas more directly to an audience, define a sense of community in terms of other experimenters as well as projected readers, or simply contextualize new poetry within literary and historical traditions familiar to a broad range of readers. As Andrews's essay demonstrates, however, these paratexts are no longer secondary background material for the poetry but forms complex enough to be analyzed as artistic experiments in their own right. Many of the paratexts have received more attention than the poetry they preface.

To analyze these text-paratext relations, my book examines the writing of six authors who represent different stages in the development of postwar paratextual poetry. It begins with Charles Olson and Jack Spicer, whose poems are accompanied by innovative notes, essays, and translation sources. It then traces the evolution of the paratext into the palimpsest source documents, essay-poem collages, and multimedia intertexts of the seventies, eighties, and nineties. These later paratexts are represented here in the compositions of Susan Howe, Charles Bernstein, Lorenzo Thomas, and Johanna Drucker. My study scrutinizes the range of divided formats in these authors' writing as texts and paratexts become increasingly interdependent and their juxtaposition creates meanings beyond those of each half individually.

Of the six poets, Olson was the one most optimistic about his ability to project an inclusive American political model through his paratextual discussions. He often inserted parenthetical comments in his poetry to suggest a communal narrative that could incorporate multiple perspectives, and his essays, which extended the scope of the parenthetical remarks, tried to present equally open-ended cultural myths of origin for his readers. Subsequent paratextual poets, in their claims about a public poetry, have expressed more concern over the fallacies and exclusions in any set of cultural myths, no matter how qualified the presentation, and they have also emphasized the likelihood of hostile or indifferent reader responses to their poetic experiments.

These authors have correspondingly foregrounded the disjunctions between the poetic text and the paratextual discussions of community and audience, even when text and paratext are in close proximity in a composition. Jack Spicer's major paratextual poetry, begun slightly after Olson's in the late fifties, is an important precursor for these later paratexts. He juxtaposed elliptical, surrealistic poetic lyrics in his books with conversational prose letters and notes that seemingly open the poetry for exegesis even as they debate the consequences of that public exposure. Among the recent authors, Susan Howe bases her poetic palimpsests upon easily recognized literary sources or on historical archives, but she fractures and revises the paratextual sources in order to retrieve moments of dissent that the narratives exclude. Charles Bernstein's essays discuss literary communities of avant-garde authors, while the poetry brings out more sharply his mistrust of any group characterizations. Lorenzo Thomas and Johanna Drucker both insert into their books popular culture–based paratextual icons and narratives, while their poetry challenges the assumptions behind the paratexts' stereotypes of conformists and outsiders.

## Theorizing an Avant-Garde: From Negation to Community

I place the paratextual discussions of community within current theoretical debates over the politics of avant-garde art. The term avant-garde, too often a generalized label for innovative writing, is used here to signify thematic and stylistic connections between paratexts in contemporary American experimental poetry and the early-twentieth-century European avant-garde manifestos.[3] If current paratexts sometimes overshadow the "central" poetic text, they are following the tradition of the visually creative prose-poetic manifestos that were often better known than the new art or poetry they introduced. And just as recent American paratexts provide a space for discussing the poetry's public, so too the early manifestos combined a call for disruptive innovation with a rhetoric of community formation and a concern for the public dissemination of the art.

The more influential aspect of the early avant-garde manifestos seems at first to be the emphasis on disruption and negation. Consider these excerpts from the manifestos of Italian Futurism, Russian Rayonism and Suprematism, Zurich Dada, and British Vorticism:

The future is behind us.
All the same we will crush in our advance all those who undermine us and all those who stand aside. (Larionov and Goncharova 88)

Let each man proclaim: there is a great negative work of destruction to be accomplished. We must sweep and clean. (Tzara 81)

BLAST years 1837 to 1900. . . . WRING THE NECK OF all sick Inventions born in that progressive white wake. (Lewis 18)

The Dadaist fights against the death-throes and death-drunkenness of his time. . . . He knows that this world of systems has gone to pieces, and that the age which demanded cash has organized a bargain sale of godless philosophies. (Ball 51)

The traditional narrative proportions (romantic, sentimental, and Christian) are abolished. . . (Marinetti 106)

One must destroy syntax and scatter one's nouns at random, just as they are born. (Marinetti 92)

I have transformed myself *in the zero of form* and have fished myself out of the *rubbishy slough of academic art.* (Malevich 118)

Although the quotes above span a six-year period beginning in 1912, their volleys sound interchangeable: declare war on a past-worshipping culture, fracture narrative and syntactic conventions, and denounce a bourgeois art of the marketplace and academy. To achieve a zero of form, the manifestos suggest a continual negation of structures in the hope that future innovators will one day destroy the work of the first generation avant-garde to make room for their own proclamations. Thus any attempt to formulate an avant-garde tradition becomes suspect.

The hyperbole of the early manifestos makes it all the more striking that their rhetoric of destruction and dispersion, and even their mistrust of popular taste, were used to project visions of ideal nations and other political communities. These communities are described in a mix of present and future tenses; even as the authors claimed to be reflecting recent technological or social changes, the purpose of the manifestos was to educate an audience to become participants in an exchange not yet realized, a new mode of artistic and political expression.[4]

The Italian poet F. T. Marinetti, in "The Founding and Manifesto of Futurism" (1909), proclaimed, "We already live in the absolute" with an age of speed and mechanization (49) while also prophesying the future state: "We will sing of great crowds excited by work, by pleasure, and by riot" (50). His manifestos emphasized the need for "artistic propaganda" (100) in order to create a new militant, anti-Romantic Italy, insisting that "art and literature exercise a determining influence on all the social classes, even the most ignorant, who drink them in through mysterious infiltrations" (100). He described the *"multiplied man"* (100), the worker who would evolve to resemble the machines he served, as if the artist could manufacture the next generation of citizens by the sheer enthusiasm of his polemics. An early supporter of Mussolini, Marinetti would nevertheless find his Futurism increasingly marginalized in Fascist politics after 1924.

The Russian Futurists and Rayonists adapted Marinetti's two-fold rhetoric of reflecting and shaping a new state. "Long live the beautiful East! . . . Long live nationality!" (90), Mikhail Larionov and Natalya Goncharova declared in 1913 as they immersed themselves in "Art for life and even more—life for art!" (89). Although they believed that the "new life requires a new community and a new way of propagation" (Zdanevich and Larionov 81), they argued that they did not need to cater to popular taste because public receptivity to their painting was inevitable: "We don't need popularization—our art will, in any case, take its full place in life—that's a matter of time" (Larionov and Goncharova 88), statements whose confidence becomes especially poignant in light of the Communists' preference for social realist art.

Among the German Expressionists, who tended more toward a cosmopolitan sense of an artists' community, Ludwig Meidner in 1914 still urged fellow artists to "start painting our real homeland," the distinctive technological landscapes of cities such as Berlin (101), while reviewer Paul Ferdinand Schmidt predicted that "Germany will be [Expressionism's] land of destiny" (15). In architecture, Walter Gropius explained the goal of the Bauhaus project in 1919 to "form a working community of leading and future artist-craftsmen" (248) for creating "Utopian" public buildings and stressed the artists' need for close "Contact with public life with the people, through exhibitions and other activities" (249). Even the international revolutionary communes projected by German Dadaists such as Richard Huelsenbeck and Raoul Hausmann were articulated as a response to the nations that had betrayed their artists' visions. "We had all left our countries as a result of the war," Huelsenbeck reminisced in 1920, denouncing the corrupt patriotism of a city like Paris "on which we had all squandered our love before the war" (23).

The relation between the avant-gardists' manifesto images of community and a political praxis has long been debated. While critics like Walter Benjamin examine connections between Futurist manifesto rhetoric and Fascism, others have dissociated the artistic avant-gardes from political movements aimed at reforming specific historical communities. Among the extended post–World War II studies of the avant-garde, Renato Poggioli examines the agonistic and nihilistic rhetoric in movements like Futurism and Dada. He concedes only a brief post-Romantic alliance between the political and the aesthetic camps of avant-gardism (12), arguing that the early-twentieth-century European movements either accepted existing political systems or dabbled in "wishful thinking" divorced from practice (95). Avant-garde art, he asserts, is characterized by a "nearly absolute unpopularity" (56), its audience an "intellectual elite" (89) composed of disparate followers who emphasize their difference from the general public (91–92).

Matei Calinescu qualifies this thesis by arguing that the disagreement between avant-gardes was over the means to effect social change:

> The main difference between the political and the artistic avant-gardes of the last one hundred years consists in the latter's insistence on the *independently* revolutionary potential of art, while the former tend to justify the opposite idea, namely, that art should submit itself to the requirements and needs of the political revolutionists. But both start from the same premise: life should be radically changed. (104)

Precisely because the aesthetic avant-gardes rejected traditional forms and transparent discourse in their attempts to revolutionize life through art, he argues, they were never simply propagandists for a specific political program (112). He insists, moreover, that the true goal of both the aesthetic and the political avant-gardes was "utopian anarchy" rather than a cohesive definition of community (104).

For Peter Bürger, the avant-gardes' politics was expressed in their critique of art's autonomous status in bourgeois society as they suggested new possibilities for social praxis by sublating life and art. He therefore focuses more on the ready-mades and performances of the Dadaists than on the earlier manifestos' political rhetoric. The avant-gardes did not fully achieve that sublation of art and praxis, he contends, and their attempts were quickly reified and imitated as an aesthetic style by would-be neo-avant-gardes. Richard Murphy has subsequently suggested that Bürger's concept of the avant-garde sublation of art and social reality still implies art's autonomous distance from the object of its critique (27). Murphy contrasts two methods of collapsing art and praxis in German Expressionist manifestos: the Romantic elevation of the social to the idealized status of art and the "'cynical' sublation" that brings art down into reality by emphasizing the disorder and fragmentation of modern life (34). The writers that he praises from the second camp, however, are those who avoided commitment to a specific social program or "*collective*" rhetoric (42).

Although these scholars of avant-garde poetics and politics treat the manifestos to varying degrees, Marjorie Perloff, in *The Futurist Moment,* incorporates some of the most extensive comparative studies of the manifesto genre among Italian, Russian, German, and British movements.[5] She emphasizes that the avant-gardes that closely associated aesthetics with utopian politics took root in countries such as Russia and Italy that were undergoing rapid industrial growth at the turn of the century (36); the authors' rupture of a mimetic art went hand in hand with militant nationalistic paeans to technology as a force that might actively restructure contemporary life. She also notes the difficulty of generalizing about the manifestos' constructions of community given their shifting claims of nationalism and cosmopolitanism, as well as the authors' different political allegiances even within the same artistic movement. What they shared was not a single goal but the form and language of the manifesto itself.

The importance of Perloff's book to a discussion of the precursors for paratexts lies in its analysis of the manifesto as a literary genre that combined provocative, imagistic prose with mass media formats to present the writers' various artistic and political agendas with broad audience appeal. The authors adapted typographic art, poetic rhythms, and narrative to the conventions of Marx and Engels's *Communist Manifesto,* a process in which, as Perloff observes, "the political manifesto is perceived aesthetically even as the aesthetic object—painting, poem, drama—is politicized" (38). The avant-garde manifestos were distributed as newspaper articles, posters, and leaflets, the proclamations sometimes appearing before the art itself. Although the world wars and political revolutions made certain aspects of Futurism, such as the celebration of militarism, impossible to duplicate, Perloff argues that the manifestos' forms and their tributes to culture-reshaping technology influenced prose texts as diverse as Roland Barthes' essay on the Eiffel Tower and the writings of American eco-artist Robert Smithson.

## American Translations

To trace the influence of European manifestos on American paratexts specifically, one must ask how the language of the European avant-gardes translated into that of literary and artistic movements in the United States, which had industrialized gradually over the nineteenth century and whose government remained stable through the world wars—a country, in other words, undergoing evolutionary rather than revolutionary changes. The American manifestos and poets' essays adapted the Futurists' mixed rhetoric of radical innovation and community formation, projecting the United States as a new artistic producer in strongly nationalistic terms. "The last few years have shown that America has a type of poetry all its own, a poetry that is as peculiar to it as the Acropolis to Athens," as well as an art of painting "conspicuously on the ascendant" (70), Marsden Hartley asserted in 1921 about the "pristine severity" of modern art experiments in an era of "mechanistic brilliance" (69). Stylistic similarities between European and

American artistic proclamations were heightened by the fact that the Italian and Russian Futurists had already imitated the expansive, celebratory language of Walt Whitman's *Leaves of Grass* in their own manifestos. But instead of the Continental rhetoric of destroying tradition, the American avant-gardes emphasized a national revolutionary tradition that needed to be reaffirmed, a paradox that is rooted in United States political history.[6]

Where the Italian Futurists, for example, spoke of a new generation of mechanized workers, as if the artists might somehow mass-produce them with their rhetoric, the United States literally had been founded by revolutionary acts of language—the Declaration of Independence, the Constitution—that needed to assume the unification and consent of the audience they sought to persuade. These documents couched rebellion in terms of rational Enlightenment discourse, concealing agency behind a language of inevitability, mixing naturalistic metaphors with ones of artifice and, in the case of the Constitution's preamble, suggestively displacing authorship to the readers who would agree to ratify its premises. The ambiguity over the authorship and authority of these textual origins is reflected in the ongoing debates over the nature of a distinctive national literature that could reassert American declarations of autonomy. In 1844, Emerson still famously lamented the absence of a representative poet: "We have yet had no genius in America, with tyrannous eye, which knew the value of our incomparable materials, and saw, in the barbarism and materialism of the times, another carnival of the same gods whose picture he so much admires in Homer" (250). While the impulse in American poetry to reaffirm cultural origins is a familiar critical thesis, Stephen Fredman points out in *Poet's Prose* that poets often address this Emersonian sense of crisis in defining a national literature in their experimental, cross-generic prose forms.[7]

One might compare, for example, the manifesto styles in issues of Wyndham Lewis's *BLAST,* the vehicle for British Vorticism, and the American journal *Contact,* edited by William Carlos Williams and Robert McAlmon. Both journals faced the difficulty of championing a native art while conceding Continental influences, and both used a revolutionary rhetoric. The difference is in their formulations of tradition. The 1914 *BLAST* manifesto, written chiefly by Lewis, declares that revolt "is the normal state" of British culture (42), yet it also stresses continuity with well-established origins. Instead of insistent attempts to redefine a uniquely British art, it alternately satirizes the national character and asserts its cultural contributions to Western civilization: "The Modern World is due almost entirely to Anglo-Saxon genius,—its appearance and its spirit" (39). Though it faults England for falling behind temporarily in the arts, it argues that new expressive forms will nevertheless "be more the legitimate property of Englishmen than of any other people in Europe" (41).

In contrast to the Vorticists' language of reclaiming a cultural birthright, William Carlos Williams's statement for the January 1921 issue of *Contact* playfully describes the journal as "the first truly representative American magazine of art" (Comment 11) at the same time that it echoes Emerson's lament for the lack of national art:

> America is far behind France or Ireland in an indigenous art. If there is no genius who can make a sermon of understanding deep enough and gentleness of sufficient catholicity to include all our animals, birds and fishes than [*sic*] those who must write, those who will create their own imaginative world as best they can with what they have, those who would meet the best in Europe with invention of their own must go down into the trunk of art, which is their word of God, where conversation can take place. (12)

Williams's second sentence, which begins as a direct paraphrase of Emerson's "The Poet," seems less certain about the origins of American genius. The mix of nature, artifice, and religion in his descriptions of a rooted "trunk of art" suggests questions of whether modern American avant-gardes should come from spontaneous improvisations or responses to previous experiments, whether the artist's work reflects a local experience or creates its own imaginative topographies, and whether a style that foregrounds artifice could still express a spiritual relation between language and American landscapes.

Williams's prologue to his prose poem *Kora in Hell* (1920), a manifesto-like preface written to give the text "a public front" (30), had already offered one response to the questions in the *Contact* editorial by combining a language of geographic rootedness with a faith in the power of the artist's imagination to transform whatever appears to be most solidly rooted.[8] The prologue pays tribute to American poets and artists but is also filled with originary moments that are adapted or reinvented, from the mention of an imaginary post-Vorticist manifesto to the "novelty" of a painted-over photographic print of Duchamp's *Nude Descending a Staircase* (9). His American landscapes begin with the memory of his mother, a Muse figure metaphorically living in her own "impoverished, ravished Eden," a fallen version of nature's nation that is nevertheless as "indestructible as the imagination itself" (7).

Gertrude Stein also associated avant-gardism with an ongoing reformulation of origins in her parodic dialogues with European manifestos in prose-poetic pieces like "Marry Nettie" (1917) or the lecture essay "Composition as Explanation" (1926). The latter portrays audiences resisting avant-garde innovations—at least until they become the new tradition: "For a very long time everybody refuses and then almost without a pause almost everybody accepts. In the history of the refused in the arts and literature the rapidity of the change is always startling" (515). She later introduced readers to her epic thousand-page *The Making of Americans* in an essay that exhorts the audience:

> Think of anything, of cowboys, of movies, of detective stories, of anybody who goes anywhere or stays at home and is an American and you will realize that it is something strictly American to conceive a space that is filled with moving, a space of time that is filled always filled with moving. (258)

This description transforms the Futurist intoxication with forward motion into an American vision of progress as a process of repetition with variation in which any foundational description must continually be rephrased.

Ezra Pound, who contributed to Lewis's BLAST, presented his own plans for an American vortex of artists and intellectuals whose productions might assert the country's cultural independence.[9] Deprecating the United States as "hardly yet a nation" in "Patria Mia" in 1913 (*Selected Prose* 101), he prophesied, "If any great city in America would tether a hundred young artists, chosen for their inventive faculties and not for their capacity to agree with contemporary editorial boards, that city could within two decades become the centre of occidental art" (140). In his "National Culture—A Manifesto 1938," he retrospectively defended the post–Civil War migration of American artists to Europe as an attempt to preserve what was left of the "revolutionary culture" of Jefferson and Adams (*Selected Prose* 161), as if the promise of that revolution had to be re-established. During the Second World War, when he delivered a series of pro-Fascist, anti-Semitic radio broadcasts from Rome in a last attempt to persuade Americans that they were fighting on the wrong side, he used the same freighted term "coherence" to rally a national audience that he would invoke to unify his vision of *The Cantos,* suggesting the audience itself as a composition to be recovered: "there must be traces of the American RACE left somewhere on the American continent. The race that set up the United States government. Have they lost all sense of coherence?" (*Ezra Pound Speaking* 47). Incoherence was the least of the charges raised against his own violent political declarations in the broadcasts, as well as in several sections of the essays and *The Cantos.*

## Afterlives of the Avant-Garde

In 1949, a committee of distinguished poets including T. S. Eliot, Allen Tate, Robert Lowell, Louise Bogan, and W. H. Auden awarded Pound's *The Pisan Cantos* the first annual Bollingen Prize for highest achievement in American poetry. Pound at the time was incarcerated in St. Elizabeths Federal Hospital, his lawyers having used an insanity defense to save him from standing trial for treason over the Rome broadcasts. Four years before the award, Harvard American-icanist F. O. Matthiessen had described the broadcasts as "a tragic instance of the consequence resulting from the gulf between poet and audience, which has been so symptomatic of recent social disequilibrium" (m17). The sheer disparity be-tween the representations of Pound as a preeminent national poet and a pariah cut off from his audience raises intriguing questions about theories of the commodification of the avant-garde. The battle within and outside the literary community over giving Pound the award and the emotion with which scholars continue to debate the relation between Pound's cultural statements and his poetry suggest that the communal vision of at least one early avant-gardist can still provoke significant controversy. Or does it simply imply that even highly disruptive political claims can be ignored or recuperated in bourgeois institutional support for the arts?

The postwar increase in awards by literary societies, universities, and publish-ing houses—including the Bollingen Prize, the National Book Awards, and the Academy of American Poets Fellowship and Lamont Poetry Selection—did sig-nal more public support networks for poets. Looking too at the popularization of specific poetic styles through anthologies and creative writing departments, as well as the limited but "stable" poetry audience suggested by post–World War II book sales from both large publishing houses and small presses, Robert von Hallberg asserts that beginning in 1960, "the poetic avant-garde was drawn into the mainstream of American literary life; since then there has been no avant-garde, though there have been poseurs" (*American Poetry and Culture* 15, 13).

The reason that we hear so many recent analyses of the death of the avant-garde, Paul Mann qualifies, is not merely because it has been institutionalized or over-theorized. The "will-to-discourse," he argues in *The Theory-Death of the Avant-Garde* (107), has always been an intrinsic part of the avant-garde project of representing resistance and otherness. He sees the manifesto genre as the site of that discursive recuperation of resistance, the public defense that "render[s] the movement indefensible" by recasting subversiveness as an aesthetic project within "conventional cultural dialectics" (108). The alternative, he suggests, might be an art associated with "silence" and "exile," a perpetual dismantling of articu-lation that cannot be advertised as a strategy (144).

The difficulty with assuming the uniform co-optation or even the theory-death of an avant-garde is that the process of its assimilation has been more com-plex and yet less totalizing than has been described. The recent experimental poetry that I discuss in this study may not have the shock quality of Duchamp's ready-mades or Marinetti's Futurist performances, and some of the later writers mock the commodity status of their own texts. All of the six focal poets have also been associated with universities or colleges. But the frequent and heated complaints about the purposeful difficulty of the poetry, however, and the fact that, for the poets after Olson, only a narrow circle of readers even within academia has been willing to read closely through their disjunctive styles, imply at least some continuing resistance to easy assimilation in these texts. The Language writers and related movements inspire authors like Dana Gioia to demand that poets "recapture the attention of the broader intellectual community by writing for nonspecialist publications," avoiding "the jargon of contemporary academic criticism" in their prose guides in favor of a "public idiom" (23). At the same time, it is the avant-gardists' paratextual discussions of theory and politics that try most energetically to engage—or educate—an audience and to define poetry's public role; many of these paratexts, moreover, have succeeded in drawing attention to the poets' agendas, even among readers impatient with the poetic styles.[10]

Part of what makes the discussion of an avant-garde poetry so contentious is that proponents of a more transparent or non-theoretical idiom for poetry and those who champion a writing style that underscores the materiality of linguistic signifiers rarely acknowledge any common ground. Accessible and plain speech are often cover terms for stylistic techniques that have become so familiar that we no longer recognize their artifice. One way to historicize the arguments over a public idiom is to look at how several of the post–World War II paratexts responded to contemporary political debates over cultural centers and margins, adapting the often contradictory evocations of an American revolutionary tradition in their own politics of poetic form.

## Avant-Garde and the Postwar Polis

The fifties are typically depicted as a decade of political consensus, and yet even the officials who strove most vigorously to define a national mission betrayed uncertainty over the nature and stability of that consensus. Senator McCarthy in 1951 could simultaneously appeal to the revolutionary fervor of the American who "has never failed to fight for his liberties" ("Conspiracy" 309) and depict a country in the last stage of self-betrayal. His speech on Communists in the State Department described "the traitorous actions" of young men "who have had all the benefits that the wealthiest nation on earth has had to offer—the finest homes, the finest college education, and the finest jobs in government we can give" ("Communists" 18), implying that the very liberality of the American lifestyle threatened the nation's survival and needed to be redefined in order to preempt conspiracies. The senator's imaginary lists of enemies and his fears of the Communist infiltration of the press contrasted with the underreporting of real internal conflicts—the initially minimal newspaper coverage, for example, of racial violence and civil rights abuse until cases like the Emmett Till murder.

Artists' essays and manifestos after 1950 reflect some of the elisions and paradoxes in these national narratives. The poet and composer John Cage, in his 1959 "Lecture on Nothing," mixes images of consensus and marginalization in his tongue-in-cheek descriptions of an "'avant-garde'" composition (*Silence* 116) in which the American political goals worth fighting for are reduced to inarticulate noises:

>                                                                Noises, too
> ,            had been dis-criminated against      ;          and being American,
> having been trained       to be sentimental,      I fought       for noises. I liked being
> on the side of the          underdog                 .
> I got police          per-mission          to play sirens.
>
> (117)

The noises themselves are portrayed as victims of prejudice; the correct "American" response, we're told, is to root for the "underdog"—while making sure beforehand that the police authorize the form of one's own protest. Cage's play with sounds and pauses asks readers to examine their own definitions of cultural noise, silence, or experimentation.

In very different formats, the poet LeRoi Jones, who grew up an avid fan of radio programs with patriotic superheroes and dark sidekicks, created satiric new narratives of nation-time for the Lone Rangers and Captain Midnights in his writing of the late fifties and early sixties. Jones, later Amiri Baraka, reinvented his persona and audience in numerous prose-poetic manifestos throughout his career, combining Futurist imagery with aesthetic and political agendas from Beat, Black Arts, and Third World Marxist movements. He turns the fifties rhetoric of consensus into a strategy for rebellion in his 1965 "State/meant," which argues, "The Black Artist's role in America is to aid in the destruction of America as he knows it" by "reflect[ing] so precisely the nature of the society, and of himself in that society," that both blacks and whites would be forced to confront the violent inequities in the status quo (169).

The uncertainty over how to articulate political centers or margins was only intensified by the cold war discourse of shifting national borders. President Eisenhower in his fifties speeches described the threat of nuclear war as a "new language" that redefined national security in terms of global power shifts ("Art of Peace" 55); protecting "the precepts of our founding documents" and making a "renewal of faith in our country" (Inaugural Address 28) now meant extending the Revolution's ideals to remote conflicts through military or economic aid. If the Korean War foregrounded the dangers and stalemates in policing these new perimeters, the U.S. involvement in Vietnam that was just beginning in the fifties would divide home audiences far more deeply by the next decade. Robert Duncan, in the preface to his war poetry in *Bending the Bow* (1968), portrayed the nation as a suspended narrative that had lost its direction. "We enter again and again the last days of our own history," he asserted, reducing the war to a contest for a "boundary we name *ours*" that is "beyond our understanding" (i). In contrast to antiwar poems that focused on message rather than style, Duncan read contemporary American politics as an entrapping form or "eternal sentence" (x) to be countered by the poet's stylistic experiments: "The pulse of this sentence beats before and beyond all proper bounds" (i).

Duncan's emphasis on an innovative *sentence* reflects the creative format of his prose preface, though its political agendas are presented more directly than in many of the poems. The antagonism that Duncan imagines between poet and audience prompts that stylistic directness. The preface depicts the readers as soldiers advancing upon protesters who plead with them to stop:

> What would I have tried to tell them? That we were unarmd? That we were not the enemy, but men of their kind? In the face of an overwhelming audience waiting for me to dare move them, I would speak to those alike in soul, I know not who or where they are. But I have only the language of our commonness, alive with them as well as me, the speech of the audience in its refusal in which I would come into that confidence. The poem in which my heart beats speaks like to unlike, kind to unkind. The line of the poem itself confronts me where I must volunteer my love, and I saw, long before this war, wrath move in the music that troubles me. (iii)

The passage, with its conflicting images of compulsion and choice (e.g., "I must volunteer my love"), captures the speaker's desire to address a sympathetic audience of peers as well as his perceived obligation to confront a larger, more hostile public. Several language models compete here as the speaker first describes an exchange in which everyone must participate, even if some of the information disturbs the listeners, and then laments the audience's "refusal" to hear the poet. The antecedent of the poet's projected "confidence" is left slightly unclear, while the convoluted syntax reinforces the difficulty of articulating that language of commonness.

The speaker's dilemma over how to define a shared communicative field signals an important difference in poets' definitions of an avant-garde community before and after World War II. For all the buried doubts about efficacy, the early European manifesto writers spoke of a new national renaissance as a ready-made construct waiting to be realized. Partly as a response to McCarthy's jingoism, as well as to modernist political rhetoric like that of Pound, the use of the first-person plural is often a highly conflicted one for American postwar poets, even for an author like Olson with close ties to modernist myth. His successors tend to posit multiple communal discourses within a culture, acknowledging consensus only in dissensus, though the discussions can sometimes trade one metanarrative for another, replacing authorizing cultural myths with new plots of subverting a dominant discourse. Bernstein in 1992 celebrates the "implicit refusal of unity," the "sharp ideological disagreements that lacerate our communal field of action" because they make contemporary American poetics "volatile, dynamic, engaging" (*AP* 1).

Changes in print technology also contributed to the proliferation of different poetry movements and critical forums. The explosion of little magazines in the sixties (e.g., the *Floating Bear, Umbra, Kulchur, "C": A Journal of Poetry, Trobar*) made possible by mimeograph, photocopying, and relatively affordable offset printing allowed poets to circulate their texts more readily outside mainstream publishing venues.[11] Language poetry originated as a series of experiments in East and West Coast little magazines of the seventies and eighties, some devoted entirely to poetics essays. The advent of electronic poetry journals has opened greater possibilities of access while making a unified reading community even more difficult to identify.

## Paratextual Poetry

Recognizing these diverse language games and audiences, one might ask, as John Ashbery did in his 1975 poem "The One Thing That Can Save America": "Is anything central?" (*Self-Portrait* 44). The heightened anxiety over how to define a public space for experimental poetry, to move beyond a small circle of fellow poets to a community of readers for those experiments, led many of the postwar Black Mountain, San Francisco, or New York avant-garde poets to create their text-paratext dialogues: poetic texts whose fractured syntax, metonymic associations, and ellipses were contextualized by extended discussions of poetic politics, references to local or national history, or reading instructions presented in more accessible formats. The early paratexts in particular often create elaborate models of community and communication using sources ranging from ancient history to tropes borrowed from field theory and systems analysis.[12] Duncan's prose-poetic preface in *Bending the Bow* mixes creation myths and particle physics to define a "commune of Poetry" (vi), while Olson crafts essays on fields and human universes. Beyond the new references, however, the key question is how the paratexts since 1950 both resemble and differ from earlier avant-garde essays and manifestos.

The reader can hear echoes of Pound's folksy tone, rapid-pace sentences, and digressiveness, for example, in Olson's prose. But the titles in Pound's criticism—"The Tradition," "How to Read," or "The Teacher's Mission"—reveal a confidence in being able to categorize the contributions to "Great literature" by the *"inventors"* and *"masters"* of each period (*Literary Essays* 23) as well as to communicate these conclusions to the receptive reader. Postwar avant-garde paratexts, while they still offer value judgments, rarely project such confidence or make such categorical claims, and neither the sources nor essays provide a straightforward explication of the indeterminate passages and lacunae of the authors' poetry.

The background information in Olson's essays, for instance, offsets some of the ellipses in his poetry but not as direct exposition. Even when presenting his poetics, many of the essays lose themselves in thematic tangents and syntactic breaks before the argument has been fully established:

> My shift is that I take it the present is prologue, not the past. The instant, therefore. Is its own interpretation, as a dream is, and any action—a poem, for example. Down with causation (except, see below). And yrself: you, as the only reader and mover of the instant. You, the cause. No drag allowed, on either. Get on with it. (*CPr* 205)

This is the opening of "'The Present Is Prologue,'" a 1952 essay that eventually provides notes on Olson's literary influences, mythological sources, and biography. Its rhythm is far closer to the manifesto form than to a conventional essay, evoking the choppy, generalized aphorisms of Pound's "VORTEX" in the 1914 issue of *BLAST:* "You may think of man as that toward which perception moves. You may think of him as the TOY of circumstance, as the plastic substance RECEIVING impressions" (153). Yet Pound's image of reception quickly gives way to one of "DIRECTING a certain fluid force against circumstance" (153), as "VORTEX" presents urgent directives and clear aesthetic genealogies. Olson, in contrast, opens with the more tentative "I take it," while words like "therefore" and "for example" (205) that suggest a structured argument only call more attention to the passage's lack of specificity. Olson instructs readers in his idea of writing as an open-ended present "action" by giving us the argumentative "shift" before the initial statement of a position and the dream-like associations without causal connections except the ones inserted by "you," the reader (205).

Olson's subversion of conventional commentary is continued in Spicer's divided poetic texts. As Michael Davidson points out (*The San Francisco Renaissance* 163), the antecedent for Spicer's bisected pages of poetry and notes in "Homage to Creeley" is Williams's *Kora in Hell,* where a prose-poetic "improvisation" is accompanied by "a more or less opaque commentary" (Williams 16) that responds to, rather than glosses, the original passage. But the reader's desire for interpretive closure becomes the overt subject of Spicer's composition. His commentator addresses the audience frequently, tantalizing us with vague insights: "There is a universal here that is dimly recognized" (*CB* 125). Although the notes provide a narrative tour of Spicer's underworld, which is modeled on the Orpheus legend, their non sequiturs, nonsense definitions, and assertions of their own falsehood celebrate the "failure" of "The Poet to bring The Poem to a close" (124), to present it as a visionary or an autotelic project.

From Spicer's misleading commentaries it is only a few steps to the paratexts collected in *The L=A=N=G=U=A=G=E Book,* an anthology of essays from various authors associated with Language writing. Despite the helpful overviews of poetic method, each statement is not only revised by the next piece but often complicated by internal shifts of approach. Barbara Barg's essay, for example, gives the reader a series of multiple choice questions instead of answers, her quiz satirizing popular assumptions about poetry:

9. Great writing occurs when the writer is
   a) young  b) recovering from a serious illness  c) "in love"
   d) "spurned"  e) exalted in mind  f) dead

(137)

The one frequently repeated message among Language authors is that political change begins with making readers interrogate the rules by which exchanges of meaning take place, whether in a literary text or the latest news sound-bite. The authors are also aware of the problems in making such claims for their writing. "I don't want to write here because I will provide in the activity of writing a rhetoric useful to the maintenance of the status quo," Brian Fawcett asserts (151) at the beginning of an essay that critiques facile claims about the political impact of disruptive literary styles, while it still envisions a poetry that might include contemporary "public language" and "*active* voices" (153).

Critical interest in these paratextual notes and essays is explained in part by the fact that their more readerly formats or familiar references provide a few guideposts for a difficult poetry. But the paratexts also take their place in the hybrid literary genres treated by postmodernist scholars: Rosalind Krauss's discussion of a "paraliterary space" in the writing of Derrida and Barthes, in which literary object and critical treatment merge into one linguistic surface (292–93) or Ihab Hassan's sketches in *The Postmodern Turn* of a "paracritical" text (118) that would suggest an awareness of its own framing fictions. The point is not only to note a blurring of genre boundaries but to look at why the divided formats of poem and paratext have persisted, even when the text and paratext are integrated in the same composition.

The paratextual poetry that I discuss has developed from dialogues between discrete texts and commentaries to include intertextual compositions whose components redefine each other's premises and forms. Recent genres in which the poet rewrites a source document, I have suggested, tend to emphasize the conflicts between text and paratext, as in the palimpsests popularized by a number of experimental American women poets. Palimpsest draws on the manifesto model of a prefacing document that is more widely recognized than the poetry it introduces. The palimpsest's source paratext is an earlier literary or historical narrative, often a canonical one with which the reader is likely to be familiar. Palimpsest thus presents an intriguing way to create a revolution-within-tradition: excerpt another author's discussions of community and then interject your own revisionary reading within the quoted language. Like the poetic essays of Olson or the Language writers, the palimpsest source provides a necessary context but does not fully explain the poet's words; the author typically plays on the disjunction between source and revision to redefine communal insiders and outcasts. Rosmarie Waldrop's *A Key into the Language of America,* for instance, revises Roger Williams's seventeenth-century text of the same name, deepening the ambiguity about an "American" linguistic heritage that is already present in his study of Narragansett vocabulary. She brackets the excerpted language from the source with multiple narrative frames, transforming Williams's text from an orderly moral about virtuous pagans who shame Christian settlers into a critical reading of both societies from the perspectives of women and immigrants.

Like palimpsest, the technique of "writing through" another author's composition employed by poets like John Cage and Jackson Mac Low also foregrounds the contemporary author's revisionary approach to a well-known source paratext. Cage's selection of excerpts from a source, for example, is determined partly by pre-set rules or by chance operations and partly by his own decisions about how much of the original line to quote; the result is a new creative text with different semantic implications and connections. Both Mac Low and Cage have chosen to write through *The Cantos* as a tribute to Pound's collage techniques—and as a tacit critique of his attempts to impose coherence in his literary and political writing.[13] Pound's name may be visually present in the capitalized letters of their compositions that spell his name, but an audience cannot hear it if a passage is read aloud. Pound's syntax and themes are fractured; there may be a design governing the initial selection of excerpts, but that design is an arbitrary one. Cage's text begins with clearly recognizable phrases from Canto I and ends with words that suggest a commentary on Pound's career ("not a trial . . . Rome baBylon no sense of / Public destrOyed" [*X* 115]), marking the failure of Pound's attempts to form a new cultural vortex.

Even the genre of translation, in which a source should be closely aligned with the poet's new text, has produced unusual text/paratext divisions in the fifties and afterward.[14] The creative mistranslations of Spicer in *After Lorca* (1957) and the Zukofskys in their homophonic *Catullus* (1958–69) influenced a generation of later writers. David Melnick's homophonic and homophile translation of the *Iliad* in *Men in Aida* uses the epic paratext to make ironic reflections on literary canons and national narratives as he re-creates the epic as a series of bawdy jokes within a gay community: "Do not sigh, gay Paris, ski up high, do say 'oh / you'" (16). Alfred Arteaga, in contrast, uses his own Spanish poem "muñeca, muñequita" (26) in *Cantos* as the paratext for a false-cognate English translation that evokes the more subtle distortions of semantic translations in which a foreign source is rearranged as a "little world-echo" of the translator's interpretive biases (27).

Many of the poets in this study experiment with the visual aspect of these text-paratext pairings, whether in the contrast between the page layouts of poetry versus poetic essay, in a divided page of poem and notes, or in the palimpsestic superimposition of one author's writing upon another's. These layouts recall the creative graphics of the early European manifestos for poetry and painting. I conclude with two authors, Lorenzo Thomas and Johanna Drucker, whose text-paratext dialogues follow the early manifestos in incorporating mass media formats and icons. The visual immediacy of the interpolated images of natives and monstrous strangers in their books contrasts with the two authors' deconstruction of narratives of either consensus or marginalization in their poetry.

Rather than impose a single framework of poetic politics on these diverse compositions, my chapters look at each author's unique constructions of community and audience address in the relation between their texts and paratexts, as well as within individual paratexts themselves. How does the poet attempt to describe or reinvent a public poetry? How does she or he move from highly specialized language games to claims made in the first person plural, and what community is denoted by that usage? By charting a wide range of paratextual forms that encourage open reader participation while they also suggest specific responses and whose directions, moreover, are matched only by their deliberate misdirections, I examine American avant-garde poetry since 1950 as a series of innovations that document their own multiple strategies of making (a)new a public space for experimental compositions.

# 2

## Parentheses and Presentation Prose: Community in Charles Olson's Paratexts

$B$y the time he was the featured first poet in Donald Allen's landmark anthology, *The New American Poetry: 1945–1960,* Charles Olson had spent a decade advocating his projective revolution in poetics. His elliptical, open-ended field compositions of archival references, anecdotes, and mythic fragments emphasized the participation of both author and audience in *"'istorin,"* an active process of investigating local events and cultural documents on one's own rather than accepting an authorized version of history.[1] Not only did Olson see this participatory poetics as a political strategy, but he strove to make his poems a "Causal Mythology," as he described it in a Berkeley lecture (*MU*1 64), a model of community that might influence its readers. Throughout his poetic career, he envisioned an American space flexible enough to redefine its borders periodically to incorporate marginal subjects and narratives. To create that communal model in his own texts, he developed two different types of paratexts: the parenthetical asides within poems that qualify and diversify his narrators' definitions of a polis and the essays that try to present myths of origin more directly to an audience.

Olson is a fascinating transitional figure to analyze in the development of postwar avant-garde definitions of a public poetry. At times, his narrators echo the rhetoric of Whitman as kosmos speaking for multitudes or Pound projecting a cultural renaissance. The hero Maximus of his *Cantos*-like poetic epic offers himself as a "lance" for social corruption (*M* 5) and a prophetic legislator for "the initiation / of another kind of nation" (633). Olson himself had firsthand experience with language as a political instrument. From 1942 to 1944, he joined a talented staff of artists and scholars at the federal Office of War Information drafting creative propaganda to persuade newly naturalized citizens to support the war effort. After the war, Olson tried to create his own small American vortex as teacher and later rector of Black Mountain College, an experimental liberal arts school in North Carolina. With a faculty that at different periods included Robert Creeley, Robert Duncan, John Cage, Franz Kline, and Merce

Cunningham, Black Mountain offered ample opportunities for artistic collaboration, though a certain cult of personality surrounded the six-foot-eight Olson who presided over his seminars like a high priest instructing disciples.

But despite his desire for community building, Olson was also deeply suspicious of attempts to articulate either a consensus or a comprehensive political agenda of one's own. Watching Ezra Pound's trial for treason, he conceded in a 1946 *Partisan Review* essay entitled "This Is Yeats Speaking" that it was "Pound's error to think, because he was able to examine with courage and criticize eloquently the world we have inherited . . . this power, necessary to us men who had to make the language new, also gave him the sight to know the cure" (*CPr* 142). Olson's own early political work had involved targeted or marginal communities as he wrote publicity for both the American Civil Liberties Union and the Common Council for American Unity, a Carnegie-funded organization founded to counter prejudice against immigrants. The threat of endangered civil liberties became very real for Olson during the McCarthy hunts for Communists in the early fifties; he was angry and frightened at being harassed by FBI agents for information about his publicity work and the activities of former colleagues.[2] With these concerns over authoritarian attempts to define loyal citizens, it is not surprising that he chose the New England seacoast town of Gloucester as the communal setting for his epic precisely because he saw it as a metaphorical island disconnected from the mainland and therefore, at least in its early stages, an independent, "heterogeneous" model for the nation (*M* 14).

Olson scholars often portray the poet as a confident didact presenting his political poetics to a select group of readers, though the lesson, paradoxically, is about the value of a dynamically open process of writing and reading that de-emphasizes the creative ego.[3] Yet Olson's most didactic challenges to the reader are themselves repeatedly qualified. In the poetry, one immediately notices the excessive use of parenthetical remarks that seems a strange verbal tic or affectation. The parenthetical asides frequently shift the terms of debate, switching pronouns, as with "(he who was I, or / is it, you?)" (*CP* 183); interpolating digressions; or simply changing tone to undercut a confident assertion, as when he writes "(. . . . 'I can be precise, / though it is no answer'" (178). These interpolated comments often express a humorous concern over the narrator's image and reception. Even the parenthetical clarifications can be as abstruse as the text, nor is it always clear why a remark falls on either side of the parentheses.

While many of Olson's poetic techniques create highly indeterminate passages as part of his process of training projective readers, these parenthetical enclosures undermine the basic distinction between a main text and readerly aside. To cite something in parentheses is to assign it secondary importance; ordinarily it can be deleted without affecting the message. But a number of his poems have more text inside parentheses than outside them, and he often uses only one parenthesis or a series of single parentheses, so that any particular comment simultaneously contributes to multiple discussions. The result is that all the perspectives given in a text are at once equally peripheral and equally necessary to the exegesis. In defending this technique to an audience, he described a *Maximus* poem that "opens with a bracket—which never ends, so it doesn't matter. . . . it just encloses everything" (*MU2* 27). The open-parenthesis poem was an ideal model for a political poetry that could incorporate multiple definitions of citizenship without prioritizing them or excluding future qualifications.

## Another Kind of Nation: From Document to Parenthesis

Olson's postwar poems, which closely link linguistic presentation with politics, suggest why and how he developed his parenthetical paratexts. His narrators associate a flat, statistical style of documentation that forecloses interpretation with a bureaucratic penchant for dehumanizing persons as enemies or casualties. In his poem "Anecdotes of the Late War" (1955), Olson blames politicians and profiteers for intensifying conflicts from the American Civil War to the present by calculating "the movement of mass of men" as nothing more than a disposable resource (*CP* 335). He found the most frightening example of this dehumanization, however, in the World War II German command. A decade earlier, when his artist friend Corrado Cagli had shown him drawings of the Nazi concentration camps, Olson wrote "La Préface," a poem that aptly prefaces his new work by asking what cultural myths a poet could still invoke after the Holocaust. Olson's modern day Odysseus is no wily hero who escapes his enemies but a No-man of "'NO RACE,'" an anonymous inmate buried under corpses and clinical statistics:

"I will die about April 1st . . ." going off
"I weigh, I think, 80 lbs . . ." scratch
"My name is NO RACE" address
Buchenwald    new Altamira cave

(*CP* 46)

With images of Buchenwald as the postmodern version of the Altamira paintings, the poet as cultural archaeologist is reduced to a cataloguer of bodies, forced to record events that he cannot prevent.

The poet had to be more than a chronicler of wastelands; the new poetry Olson had begun to imagine would use a method of inclusive parenthetical documentation. He gives a self-conscious example of the technique in "La Préface":

Birth in the house is the One of Sticks, cunnus in the crotch.
Draw it thus: (   ) 1910 (

It is not obscure. We are the new born, and there are no flowers.
Document means there are no flowers
                    and no parenthesis.

It is the radical, the root, he and I, two bodies
We put our hands to these dead.

The closed parenthesis reads: the dead bury the dead,
                    and it is not very interesting.
Open, the figure stands at the door, horror his
and gone, possessed, o new Osiris, Odysseus ship.
He put the body there as well as they did whom he killed.

                                                    (*CP* 47)

The passage in fact seems deliberately convoluted, partly because of the arcane
Tarot card imagery but more so because of its contrast with the earlier statistical
details. The documentary numbers associated with the camp inmates are replaced
by a single date that lacks a referent and is surrounded by empty or unclosed
parentheses.[4] To supply one reference, 1910 is the year "he and I," Olson and
Cagli, were born; to fill in the blank parentheses with names and to close them
with another date would turn this into a tombstone line marking the artists' death.
But when the parenthesis is left "Open," the Odysseus "figure stands at the door"
of different narrative possibilities: "o new Osiris, Odysseus ship," images of res-
urrection and mythological journeys. The blurring of the hero with his "ship" is
a gentle rebuke to Pound, who described the poet as an authority prescribing
cultural axioms for his audience in "I Gather the Limbs of Osiris." Olson's hero
will not be the controlling ego but the vessel of a poetry that continually adjusts
its definitions of cultural centers. In the insistence on making contact with the
dead, whom the poem describes as "unburied," Olson's narrator emphasizes that
these communal redefinitions are not an act of forgetting past atrocities but a
critical interrogation of how they occurred and who was complicit in the con-
voluted chain of violence suggested in the passage: "He put the body there as
well as they did whom he killed."

Olson's narrators after World War II increasingly qualify their assertions of
political community in parenthetical paratexts. Some achieve that effect with a
few strategic interpolations. In the 1950 poem "Bigmans II," for example, the
title character is a frontier hero who sees "his job as civilizer" building city walls
in territories "new enough to wipe out wrongs" (*CP* 150). The narrator exhorts
his audience to learn from Bigmans's example (149). Yet he juxtaposes his praise
for the strength of the hero's "inner wall" around the city with an enclosure in

the poetic line, the parenthetical comment "(which none can equal yet)" (150) that hints at the possibility of future rivals to Bigmans and alternate communities. We learn that Bigmans's countrymen, like Gilgamesh's subjects, are praying for such a rival to challenge the hero whose presence they find too imposing.

Bigmans, as the name suggests, is a variant of Maximus, the protagonist of Olson's epic poem also begun in 1950. Olson expresses the need for inclusivity in this national narrative by weaving some of his most intricate parenthetical layering into its series of letter-poems. The narrator in "Letter 3" presents the audience with an independent community modeled on Gloucester as a version of a Greek city-state:

> Polis now
> is a few, is a coherence not even yet new (the island of this city
> is a mainland now of who?  who can say who are
> citizens?
>
> (*M* 15)

The speaker first limits his city-state to the privileged "few" that follow his quest, the vision of a utopian "coherence not even yet new" evoking Pound's vocabulary of coherence and making it new. But the desire for coherence is interrupted, thematically and grammatically, by the parenthetical redefinition of the community as a set of questions: "a mainland now of who? who can say who are / citizens?" Olson's narrator delights in breaking all the rules—leaving the syntax ambiguous, refusing to close the parentheses, and deleting the initial capitalization that separates one sentence from another—in order to confuse the distinction between island and mainland and to emphasize that his symbolic Gloucester will never achieve formal closure about its requirements of citizenship.

Continuing the open parenthetical comment in the next verse paragraph, the narrator argues that the individual listener alone can negotiate definitions of citizenship:

> Only a man or a girl who hear a word
> and that word meant to mean not a single thing the least more than
> what it does mean (not at all to sell any one anything, to keep them anywhere,
> not even
> in this rare place
>
> (*M* 15)

The lawgiver's ability to persuade these listeners with his undistorted "word" is undercut by the insistent repetition of "mean" that already invites slightly different interpretations of its semantic nuances. The second parenthetical remark puts that anxiety over semantic slippages in perspective. The real distortion is

not the poet's attention to breaks and slippages in meaning but the slickly pack-
aged community model that a demagogue might try to sell a prospective resi-
dent, "us[ing] words cheap" and men even more cheaply (13) without a sense of
their histories; this is the "pejorocracy" (7) or inferior rule that Olson sees domi-
nating the nation.

Olson's polis, in contrast, is the site of an already contentious history that he
"unburies," to borrow the language of "La Préface," in layer after parenthetical
layer. In "Letter 2," when the narrator probes Gloucester's "(hidden / city" on a
historical tour (*M* 9), he describes quarters for black servants in the nineteenth
century and thinks back to the merchants who "hid, or tried to hide, the fact
the cargo their ships brought back / was black (the Library, too, possibly so
founded)" (9).[5] The open-parenthesis phrase "(hidden / city" graphically sug-
gests both the separation of the servant quarters from the main houses and the
underlying connection between the early slave trading and the community that
profited from it (9). The remark that the Library might have been founded with
those profits only heightens the irony; the concealed act may literally underwrite
the public's reading material. In "Letter 14," which also mentions slave trading,
Olson presents a composite history of violence and profiteering in the New World
as the backdrop for a series of parenthetical addresses moving from "(Cape Ann
. . .)" and "(Gloucester!)" to "(o America)" and "(o you Americans)" (68), ad-
dresses that figuratively frame the nation with a Melvillean narrative of "moral
struggle" (66) rather than Whitman's celebratory catalogues. This is not a con-
tradiction in Olson's model polis; while he still sees part of Gloucester's history
as a defiance of "nascent capitalism" (105), that resistance only has meaning
against its internal and external threats.

To look at how these parenthetical historical debates extend to Olson's por-
traits of a contemporary poets' community, one can compare the early images
of Gloucester's shores with a coastal metaphor from a late *Maximus* poem in 1966.
The poem is a succession of lengthy passages introduced by single parentheses,
a form that seems appropriate to its discussion of the waves of immigrants to
reach America:

>           my father a Swedish
> wave of
> migration after
> Irish? like Negroes
> now like Leroy and Malcolm
> X the final wave
> of wash upon this
> desperate

ugly
cruel
Land this Nation
which never
lets anyone
come to
shore: Cagli said

(*M* 496–97)

The excerpt, taken from an extended parenthetical remark about Olson's boyhood trip to Plymouth, is not only unusually straightforward but it risks sounding trite, with the liberal poet thinking of the original settlers and denouncing prejudice or assuming that these ethnic groups all faced comparable difficulties.

This is a more complex statement of poetic and political community, however, than it seems. By linking the poet LeRoi Jones (later Amiri Baraka) with Malcolm X, Olson implicitly asserts the political impact of poetry. Jones, who had just begun to advocate a Black Nationalist art, now precedes the assassinated leader as if he were taking up his labor. Placing Jones in a poem with extended single parentheses also recalls the fact that Jones had adapted this technique in his own early poetry. Where the nation failed to incorporate its black poets, Olson suggests that these parenthetical lines were indeed inclusive enough to express the New York poet's very different visions of a polis. Olson reinforces the connection by commenting, later in the passage, that both his own father and the father of "Leroy" were postal workers in small towns; the two sons inherit the symbolic responsibility of spreading American letters from outposts. A sense of irony, moreover, pervades the lament about who is really at the marginal shore of American culture; Jones, since 1959, had helped to publicize Olson by printing several of his more experimental texts in little magazines such as *Kulchur* and *Yugen*.[6] As a final ambiguity, the placement of Corrado Cagli's name directly after this passage makes it unclear whether he or Olson characterizes the nation as an unfriendly mainland. One comes to an American "shore" not through acts of assimilation, as the immigrant metaphor initially suggested, but through interchanges at the borders of a polis in which each speaker's relative displacement is always contrasted with that of other liminal language users.

By playing on these parenthetical shifts in perspective, Olson avoids simply equating the situations of his different marginal characters. Yet even in the opening *Maximus* poems, he explores the possibility of building a bridge between islands of isolated or overlooked narratives, describing the Gloucester-man in parentheses as part of an "American / braid" linked "with others like you" (7–8). While the poems in the first volume stay fairly close to Gloucester's landmarks and history, some of Olson's most ambitious early searches for myths of origin take place in his prose essays and lectures.

### "'Presentation' Prose"

Just as the parenthetical remarks in the poetry undermine the distinction between main text and aside, so too these essays are no longer a clearly secondary supplement to the poetry but rather creative extensions of Olson's poetic forms. Olson used similar techniques of parenthetical qualification, digression, and metonymic connections in both genres. In 1951, he offered a selection of poems and essays and "a verse-prose" composition to the editor of *Origin* with the comment that these new pieces "all go together. Thus, you can select or order or re-order with no anthological problems! This is all, all, one face of the character, olson!" (*LO* 25).

The essays are highly self-qualified because they take up the poetry's challenge of theorizing nonexclusive myths of origin for a polis, a desire reflected in ambitious titles like "Human Universe" and "The Gate and the Center." On the whole, however, the essays are not only more expansive in scope than many of the individual early *Maximus* poems but provide more intermediary steps in their associative leaps of logic. Where the poetry tends to be elliptical and fragmented, juxtaposing facts without transition, the essays detail their sources at greater length, presenting arcane scholarship through traditional tropes of American literary history: city-states on a hill, glyphic landscapes, and noble natives. The prose balances semantic indeterminacy with a stronger sense of presence as presentation: the need to make author and audience respond to each other. Many of the essays, described by Olson as "'presentation' prose" (*LO* 90), originated as actual letters to friends. I include in this discussion a number of Olson's lectures, couched in his trademark allusive style, that introduced his poetry and its sources to specific audiences.

"I feel so gaddamned pushed to EXPLICITNESS," Olson wrote to Creeley in 1952, concerned that his writing might be too abstract to reach an audience beyond his immediate correspondents (*Charles Olson and Robert Creeley* 142). His essays and presentations coax, challenge, and question their readers as if asking for an affirmation of textual claims, even when he was well established as a public figure. Olson's Beloit College lectures in 1968 are entitled "Poetry and Truth," suggesting absolute values, but they are continually punctuated by anxiety over communication: "So that I really do mean truth. . . . Can you hear me? I do mean truth, and in a very simple sense. I hope I even have my definition of it" (*MU2* 7). He told the audience that he wanted to provide "a living exegesis" so that they "understood every word" of the poetry he read, making his language "Completely penetrable to your mind, to your life, to your thought, to your feelings" (50).

## The New Manifesto

Throughout his career, Olson used a variety of prose paratexts in order to create that reading context for his poetry. "Projective Verse," published in *Poetry New York* in 1950, is perhaps Olson's best known essay, modeling its reader address on the turn-of-the-century avant-garde manifestos. It denounces "'*closed' verse*" and the neo-Romantic "'*Egotistical Sublime*'" of contemporary lyrics, exhorting poets to continue the "revolution of the ear, 1910" with a "COMPOSITION BY FIELD" (*CPr* 239) in which the poet would be radically open to new perceptions and his kinetic art would become a high "energy-discharge" from author to reader (240). The language of "Projective Verse" seems an exuberant reflection of that energy transfer, its sentences cluttered with capital letters and exclamation points. Olson's headlong impressionistic style recalls the pace of images in the prewar avant-garde manifestos, designed to carry the reader off with their enthusiasm.

But Olson revises the Futurists' militantly antagonistic sense of community. War, in Marinetti's manifestos, is "the world's only hygiene" (50) because it forces the emergence of a powerful new Italy as a subject for art and poetry. Olson's own manifesto qualifies the violence of the Futurist revolution in favor of persuading and expanding an existing circle of writers and sympathetic readers. He establishes this in the sequential definitions of "projective" in the essay's first line, each word set off by a single parenthesis mark:

(projectile    (percussive    (prospective

(*CPr* 239)

If the verse is first suggested as a weapon in "(projectile," the second term, "(percussive," makes the description more ambiguous; do we hear the rattle of machine-gun fire or merely musicians' drumming? The final description of "projective" verse is simply "(prospective," a neutral term that leaves its completion open for further commentary without specific parameters. When Olson returns to the image of a weapon later in the essay, it is only to shoot down "rhetorical devices" instead of enemies (243). The central machine in this statement of poetics is the typewriter, which Olson praises for its ability to create "multiple margins, to juxtapose" ideas (246) rather than to prioritize them.

There is also a shift in tone from the Futurists; "Projective Verse," upon close scrutiny, is both more expository and yet more conditional than a manifesto. Olson uses fewer fanciful metaphors, and his narrator is a cross between a schoolmaster and a tour guide: "I return you now to London, to beginnings, to the syllable, for the pleasures of it" (*CPr* 245). But he provides only generalized references about "a stance toward reality outside a poem" (246) that might connect the poet's work to a broader field of action. The clarity is further compromised, moreover, by a tendency to over-qualify abstract instructions for the reader's benefit. Olson lightens his own pronouncements by self-parody, as when he banters, "So there we are, fast, there's the dogma" (240) or else modifies his claims so thoroughly in parenthetical asides as to forestall objections: "(The [projective] stance involves, for example, a change beyond, and larger than, the technical, and may, the way things look, lead to new poetics and to new concepts from which some sort of drama, say, or of epic, perhaps, may emerge.)" (239). By the end of the sentence, it would be difficult to imagine a more uncontroversial message for a manifesto or a more tentative prelude to a national epic.

The message, ultimately, may be less important than the speaker's insinuating address to the audience as he slips between "I" and "we" voices with his parenthetical remarks—directions such as "(We now enter, actually, the large area of the whole poem . . .)" (*CPr* 243); over-solemn promises of "(I swear it)" (242); or humorous requests for help with a definition: "(. . . pass me that, as Newman Shea used to ask, at the galley table, put a jib on the blood, will ya.)" (244). This *Maximus*-like shipboard slang suggests that his readers have become his sailing mates. If such remarks do not fully clarify the arguments, they at least create the impression of a special contract between author and reader. When the poet shares the "secrets" gained by his willingness to regard himself as an object among other natural objects, he is most fully utilized "by himself and thus by others" (247); not only will the poetry be able to "carry much larger material" on the scale of epic (248), but as Olson implies in the metaphor of poetry as speech act, he may have an audience to respond to that epic.

## Deferred Definitions

Olson never abandoned the premise of a public contract, a rhetoric of addressing and reshaping an entire polis in his writing. A contract does not insure textual transparency; Olson warns that the reader will have to go "wading through unconscionable stuff" to keep up with him (*CPr* 304), evaluating the multiple histories he sketches for his models of poetic community, each founding narrative or definition more inclusive than the last.

Olson's essay "Human Universe," published in 1951–52 in the journal *Origin,* offers an ambitious overview of Western theories of language and epistemology that exemplifies both the scope and the difficulty of his abstract genealogies. Where "Projective Verse" opens with percussive noises and a dramatic note about "Verse now, 1950" (*CPr* 239), this essay's introduction sounds like the middle of an argument whose points of contention we have missed:

> There are laws, that is to say, the human universe is as discoverable as that other. And as definable.

The trouble has been, that a man stays so astonished he can tri-
umph over his own incoherence, he settles for that, crows over it,
and goes at a day again happy he at least makes a little sense. Or, if
he says anything to another, he thinks it is enough—the struggle does
involve such labor and some terror—to wrap it in a little mystery:
ah, the way is hard but this is what you find if you go it.
The need now is a cooler one, a discrimination, and then, a shout.
(*CPr* 155)

These opening sentences are so general in their self-reflexive description of
communication as a struggle that they become a parody of nonexclusiveness,
likelier to frustrate than to engage a reader. Olson defers the promised laws, dis-
coveries, and definitions or else provides comparisons in which the points of
reference are not specified. For persistent readers who appreciate the "labor" and
"mystery" as part of the projective learning process, the rest of the essay devel-
ops the opening terms through a kind of regressive association that enacts Olson's
critique of descriptive labels. He links "discrimination" to the classical logos as
discourse (155) and then to logic, classification, and idealism (156), while the
"shout" is language as a spontaneous speech act, a discussion that leads him to
speculate about the possibility of phenomenal "discovery" (156) and the origi-
nal "unselectedness" or flux of human experience (160).

When I argue that Olson's essays are not simply explanatory poetics statements
in a conventional sense, it is because of this technique of explication as deferral,
where the series of qualifications increases the reader's eagerness for the original
event or legend that can sum up all the intermediate references. Olson's deferred
definitions and his critique of the transcendental Logos seem the most post-
modern aspects of his essay style. Unlike Derrida's sense of *différance*, however,
Olson's word games do not break down into a free play among signifiers.

## The Communal Myth of Poetic Language

If no single term or legend is sufficiently inclusive to provide a common origin
for his polis, the closest Olson comes to a definition of mythology is the con-
cept of poetic language itself as the participatory art form shared by a culture. In
the short 1952 essay "'The Present Is Prologue,'" Olson's reference to a mytho-
logical past inspires a discussion of "the poems and the inscriptions" from cul-
tures like the ancient Sumer (*CPr* 206), suggestively equating some of the earli-
est writing with forms of poetry. He later rephrases his literary archaeology as a
search for "writing and acts" (207); the link between writing and action is cru-
cial since Olson's essays will define mythology both as a poetic expression and a
political activity.

He makes that connection in the Berkeley lecture entitled "Causal Mythology" (1965) by arguing for poetry's ability to reflect the *"imago mundi,"* a shared perception of the earth and of the archetypal city that all humans instinctively possess: "That *that's* initial in any of us. We have *our* picture of the world and *that's* the creation" (*MU*1 94). Analyzing the *imago mundi* and the ways in which contemporary political systems distort it, he insists, is a type of activism. The "invention," he begins and then corrects himself, "the *discovery* of formal structural means is as legitimate as—*is* for me the form of action" (94). By invented/discovered structures, he evokes both his own poetic forms as they try to re-create a model of language exchange within the ideal city and the imperfect "structure" of the bureaucratic "establishment" he has just been criticizing (94). "Put an end to nation, put an end to culture, put an end to divisions of all sorts" (94) that artificially separate members and outsiders, Olson urges readers, encouraging them to imagine the "city of the earth" as the new vision of John Winthrop's "'city on a hill'" (79).

Olson's lecture foregrounds the conflict within his concept of mythological language over the relative status of the poetic text that *enacts* a causal mythology and the paratextual commentary that explains that poetic process. He defines a causal mythology as something meaningful in itself without extraneous comparison or interpretation: *"that which exists through itself is what is called meaning"* (*MU*1 64). The excerpts from *The Maximus Poems* that Olson read in this lecture seem to make such claims for their own projections of "the history / of the nation" (*MU*1 71), and yet Olson framed his poetry reading with numerous asides about the "real," "factual," or "original" nature of the poetic text as if he needed to validate the poetic claims through the commentary. He read aloud twice a *Maximus* poem that proposes "to build out of sound the wall / of a city" (*MU*1 65), like Amphion piping stone walls into place in the myth of Thebes. In between the two readings, Olson reproduced a rhetoric of verbal city-building that is directly linked to the perceived accessibility of his audience address: "I want to go back now, really building, coming back to that original poem that I read. In fact, I'm really trying to explain that I don't believe I'm obscure" (*MU*1 69).

If he protests a little too strongly, this defensiveness about obscurity sums up the mythologist's dilemma: no poetic text has meaning solely in itself when the poet must take into account an audience's possible response and make a paratextual case for the significance of his verbal strategies. A poet's lecture, arguably, predetermines a format of readings interspersed with exegesis, but many of Olson's essay paratexts also present causal myths in divided formats that intersperse poetic lines, diagrams, and lists with more conventional explanatory passages, each part augmenting the others' presentations.

## Convention Halls and Libraries: Olson's American Spaces

Olson's hope of inaugurating a new national experiment through these text-paratext relations may seem tenuous, and yet his use of prose texts to discuss the search for foundational myths, as Stephen Fredman observes, may be the most American aspect of his compositions.[7] Olson was acutely aware of what I have described as an American revolutionary tradition of re-creating origins, particularly in the idea of founding documents that presume the authorizing support of readers. His Office of War Information specialized in this type of circular logic; the bilingual pamphlet that he helped to produce, *Spanish Speaking Americans in the War,* enlisted the support of its target audience by asserting that the Hispanic community was already contributing heavily to the war effort. The pro-immigrant Carnegie journal *Common Ground,* on which he had worked as an editorial assistant, had used similar persuasive techniques, showcasing writing by immigrant authors to "encourage the growth of an American culture which will be truly representative of all the elements that make up the American people." The distinctions between *culture* and *people* and between *encouraging* and *representing* ethnic diversity reflect the contradictions of a forum that presented its heterogeneous America as something already known to, and accepted by, the journal's readers, despite the anti-alien sentiment of the period.

Olson's goals for his own writing are less bluntly stated, but many of the essays and lectures argue for the poetry's communal images and stylistic challenges as devices simultaneously innovative and familiar. "Projective Verse" at one point asks readers to accept a poetic technique as an established "convention" so that "the revolution out of which it came" may be more widely publicized (*CPr* 246). As a prelude to reading an excerpt from the *Maximus* section "Making a Republic on Watchhouse Point" in his "Poetry and Truth" lectures, Olson examined the poet's drive to "make our image of a union of ourself" (*MU2* 27), the use of "ourself" summing up the ambiguity over whether that image of union is a personal fiction or a collectively supported expression. In a less-than-sober reading at Berkeley, he alternately described the lecture room as a "convention hall" (*MU1* 97) in which he might win over an audience and assumed his own election, declaring that poets are acknowledged "political leaders today" (112).

As early as "A Bibliography on America for Ed Dorn," a letter-essay first written in 1955 to one of his students, Olson presented his creative guide to the nation as a history already familiar to the addressee. Under the category of "Person," Olson offered this poetically irregular "book": "simply that you has this ADVANTAGE, that you is an american," with the parenthetical remark: "(no patriotism intended: sign reads, 'LEAVE ALL FLAGS OUTSIDE. . . .')" (*CPr* 301). This lower-case "american" textual space is marked by verbal signs that try to deny their status as artificial signifiers ("'LEAVE ALL FLAGS OUTSIDE'") as if they could directly incorporate the persons of the readers without any mediation. "You" are invited to enter the enclosure because you already have the "ADVANTAGE" of citizenship. But how does the poet-historian delineate an American advantage without the reductive flag-waving that he denounced in *The Maximus Poems*?

As the bibliographic title suggests, Olson gives his audience his own prodigious reading material as founding documents for a reformed republic, just as he had earlier offered Melville's library as the background for an American "SPACE" in *Call Me Ishmael* (*CPr* 17). A number of Olson's essay paratexts are little more than poetically arranged lists of anthropological, philosophical, and literary texts intended for friends or students. "A Bibliography on America" maps out a national geography as a feast of written resources to be digested by the reader: "Mr Melville, how to cook a whale; Professor Merk, how pemmican was born; how to skin a buffalo" in a text by Stanley Vestal (302), followed humorously by a mention of Olson's own poetry. Instead of mimicking Pound's canons of "'grrrate bookes'" (301), however, the "Bibliography" diet is deliberately difficult to consume with the narrator's parenthetical digressions in the middle of authoritative citations, his critical stance toward several sources, and his omission of book titles altogether at points in the discussion, prompting the reader to "find em yrself" (304). By substituting such an elliptical bibliography for an essay overview, Olson plays the self-absenting didact, refusing to summarize the disparate texts as a coherent cultural history. Instead, he uses the research sources in his paratexts to offer displaced or translated myths of origin for the nation. I would like to look at two of Olson's letter-essay series, one from an early fifties publication and the other from a mid-sixties teaching guide, to suggest the range of his paratextual experiments with different roles for the poet and the reader in creating his own versions of an American revolutionary tradition.

## A Mayan Universe

The poetic prose of *Mayan Letters* (1953) was part of a correspondence with poet Robert Creeley during Olson's amateur investigations of sites in the Yucatán in 1951. Olson, who had kept carbon copies of his letters,[8] prompted Creeley to edit a selected volume for publication, and Olson also revised excerpts from the letters in his essay "Human Universe." He draws upon reference histories, legends, and his own interpretations of hieroglyphic artifacts in these letters to speculate enthusiastically about the ancient Maya as a civilization in which the "TOP CLASS" were cultural scholars (*ML* 31). Olson uses the Maya both as a non-European example from which to critique the "mis-centered" role of the subject in western humanism (64) and as a source that does not limit American history solely to the United States. These letters focus on the poet's role in a community, depicting poetry as a model that not only represents an inclusive polis but may help to perpetuate it.

Olson believed that Mayan hieroglyphs and art were a form of "verse" (*ML* 42) that represented the artists' perceptions of the *"human figure"* (65) juxtaposed with the "expression & gesture of all creatures" and were also an "intimate" medium (41).[9] The combination was irresistible for a poet who wished to make the most inclusive definition possible of a polis while still retaining his readers' focused attention. His argument in "Human Universe" that the "love and flesh" of the contemporary Maya now provide the only remaining "sign" of that original culture (*CPr* 158) manages to suggest both an absence and a powerful continuity. The artistry of the early makers still persists in descendants who have become living embodiments of the glyphic representations of an inclusive polis: "they wear their flesh with that difference which the understanding that it is common leads to" (158). This body politic remains open enough to incorporate the alienated North American poet who had doubted his "rights"—a suggestively political term—to his physical "organism" (158) and also his relation to his own American polis. The tribute to the Maya becomes a covert self-tribute, for in articulating their latter-day community, Olson places himself in the descriptive public role of the original glyph writers.

In an attempt to capture what he saw as the expressive range of the glyph artists, Olson not only includes his own drawings of artifacts in *Mayan Letters* but intersperses the prose passages with poems and parenthetical comments as if he were charting a series of causal mythology dialogues on the pages for his correspondent. He qualifies his interpretations of the glyphs and legends with multiple asides that insist on the immediate, changeable nature of his communication. He begins one passage, "fr the way it looks today," and then he catches himself: "(i mean precisely today, things keep shifting so as i cut away at my ignorance)" (*ML* 54). Another letter that opens dramatically with an invocation of Mayan ceremonies closes with a poem that recontextualizes a mythic word-giver as a less-distanced "interlocutor" (51). Even in "Human Universe," which has a more conventional visual layout, the essayist tries to translate the memory of the glyphs into a direct appeal to his contemporary readers: "O, they were hot for the world they lived in, these Maya, hot to get it down the way it was—the way it is, my fellow citizens" (*CPr* 166).

How applicable did Olson find these Mayan analogies for his own communal politics? The touch of bravado in the "Human Universe" address to "fellow citizens" concludes the essay on the note of a public speech. But Olson also describes these citizens paradoxically as "natural children" of an unnatural, materialistic culture antithetical to that of the Maya (*CPr* 158), nor is he always certain of his own cultural translations. The excited tone of the *Mayan Letters* is broken by passages that do not merely qualify but challenge or suspend the poet's role as archaeologist offering the reader a rediscovered *imago mundi*. In this excerpt, for example, Olson interrupts his argument about Mayan visual symbols that represented the identity of an entire community:

> precisely what
> they needed, was
> the image of
> (Well! To hell with that. Pardon me. Get up off my
> face, olson.)
> themselves

> (*ML* 33)

When the colloquial Americans insert themselves parenthetically here in the Maya's self-representations, it seems less like a revisionary addendum than an intrusion. Olson links this sudden sense of being an intruder in the mythic histories he borrows to the suspension of his own lecture as he imagines that even a sympathetic reader may be growing impatient with his style. The United States translation of Kukulkan, the Mayan mythic hero who spread their language to other cultures, is lowercase "olson" who satirizes the earnestness of his struggle to reform his polis.

### "America *Already Has* Plenty of *History*": *Pleistocene Man*

In contrast to the *Mayan Letters,* Olson's 1968 composition *Pleistocene Man* emphasizes the reader as the cultural archaeologist. This piece was originally a series of teaching letters written three years earlier to John Clarke, who was taking over a class from Olson, a context that may have heightened the symbolic play on the didact's absence. Yet despite the textual ellipses and indirections, Olson presents a national declaration of independence here, a declaration grounded in a period long before nationalism.

In order to make that assertion, Olson drew on his interest in the work of geographer Carl Ortwin Sauer, whose research included studies of New World prehistory.[10] Sauer wrote about human settlements in America as far back as the Pleistocene period, an early presence that moves Olson to declare in *Pleistocene Man* that "America doesn't need to be the *equal* of Europe" any longer (20):

> And I can confidently ASSURE YOU
> AMERICA *ALREADY HAS*
> PLENTY OF *HISTORY*
> for us to use our abstract powers
> ON: Sauer say on

Pleistocene Man under
the edge of the ICE
   Northern
     Michigan
        Iowa Sub-stage
        of Wisconsin De-
   GLACIAL

                                                     (8)

This passage presents a unique version of a founding history that must be approved by its readers. Pleistocene culture in America, as Olson playfully implies in the increasingly indented lines of this geography, is indeed marginal, formed at the edges of the glaciers shifting across the continent. Unlike more familiar narratives of pilgrim settlers and other immigrants, the Pleistocene is a founding epoch so distant that it becomes a source for common "use" by readers, a prehistory to be articulated now by "our abstract powers" of myth-making. Indeed, "we" may be able to produce a myth more accurate than many of the contemporary textbooks, Olson offers, noting that few American references except for Sauer's provide the thesis about Ice Age man in the New World (6).

As the creative lineation suggests, Olson once again associates the use of poetic language with a representation of cultural origins,[11] but he focuses here on the reader's response to that language. Whereas the narrator in "Human Universe" still needs to interpret Mayan hieroglyphs for his audience, the persona in *Pleistocene Man* collapses the distinction between prehistoric artifacts and postmodern inscriptions by presenting his own writing as a direct reenactment of Paleolithic culture:

> Don't read this as a letter : read it as though I were
>    —as in fact  etc—*Paleolithic* !

Jack—
   It's almost like poetry. In fact it *is* poetry, Pleistocene, in that simplest *alphabetic* sense, that you can learn the language of being alive—in that most elementary way which is so easily taken for granted (or used as though it were only elementary)—that with which you are most familiar—as though you were learning to read and to write for the first time. (9)

The author is transformed from a cultural didact into an artifact; his writing and his persona seem interchangeable as he becomes a part of the origin he describes when he asks his addressee to read the text "as though I were / —as in fact etc—

*Paleolithic* !" The reader must recover the poet's displaced traces through his paratextual commentary, a point that Olson underscores by associating this more familiar prose letter format with a type of Pleistocene "poetry."

Olson's insistence on the "elementary" nature of his references to carvings or cave paintings in his analogy of "learning to read and to write for the first time" or simply of reexperiencing a shared "language of being alive" deserves careful attention. In what sense is either the material or his presentation an elementary alphabet? Even if one reads his account of the Pleistocene experience as a metaphor for a profound receptivity at the most basic level of human perception,[12] that responsiveness is being prompted here through a curriculum of complex source texts and mediated specifically by Olson's prose-poetic sequences, which can hardly be described as transparent. If his essay is a model for introducing the Pleistocene's "poetry" to an audience, then it heightens the boldness of his assertion that extended exegesis is not only unnecessary but harmful, since every student should be trained to find his way through the visual or textual archives (*PM* 12). "Don't," he cautions Clarke simply, "do anyone else's work for them" (12).

Olson still denounces the American pejorocracy as vigorously as ever in *Pleistocene Man,* but its hope that the *"growing"* generation of humans (16) may be able to put together the "few, and *separable,* remains" (13) of either prehistoric finds or postmodern lecture fragments creates a frame for the late *Maximus* poems. The entries of the third *Maximus* volume, arranged posthumously by Olson's editors, oscillate between visions of a polis bounded by a "non-niggardly definition" of city walls (*M* 633) and portraits of a local and national community fallen into chaos. While it is difficult to speculate about the direction the epic might have taken had he lived longer, the sixties essays and lectures offer a final version of Olson's parenthetical asides to an audience about that project. The continuing concern over communication in many of the late prose paratexts derives from the fact that Olson presents their increasingly ambitious and abstract outlines, notes, and curricula as the provisional scaffolds for new communal mythologies whose language of the true or real ultimately must be confirmed by the listener. As the provocation for that confirming or qualifying response, the paratext itself, as *Pleistocene Man* suggests, becomes an integral part of the poem as political causal mythology.

Olson did not take audience participation for granted in either his sixties or his fifties paratexts. He complained in a 1969 interview that as a poet "you can't do anything but be the piper of a sleeping nation" (*MU*2 152). But the hope of awakening active readers was the only defense he saw against political enclaves that were neither benevolent nor participatory and that deliberately concealed themselves from the public. While Olson may have integrated "hidden" histories in his early Gloucester chronicles, he presented a more sinister parenthetical city in "A Bibliography on America for Ed Dorn": "as of America (and I can't tell you where to go for it, simply that I imagine it's a law . . . that the real *power* contemporary to one is *kept hidden*)" behind its wealth or lobbies (*CPr* 309). The poet "can only hack away" at uncovering those concealed centers, Olson confesses. "And read between all lines" (310).

The paratexts that read between Olson's own poetic lines continue to draw attention to the models of a polis in his corpus as a whole. "Projective Verse" has become a touchstone postwar American poetry manifesto, while the amount of critical attention to his other essay paratexts suggests that one of Olson's chief legacies is the creative paratextual forum for defining an audience, a political agenda, or an alternate canon while championing a poetry that disrupts the premise of an authoritative history or a transparent message. This forum is all the more noticeable in Olson's corpus because few of the recent poets who use paratexts share his optimism that any mythic or historical frameworks, however provisional, can incorporate the diverse marginal perspectives in a nation. Olson's own textual polis is hardly immune to this problem; women, for example, remain little more than archetypal fertility figures or malign sorceresses in both his poetry and paratexts.[13]

I have argued that many contemporary American avant-garde poets tend to fracture and revise their paratextual sources and to foreground the contradictions involved in explicating a radically disjunctive poetry. Yet their poetry is also increasingly dependent upon these paratexts, both for contact with a potentially wider audience and as a way of asserting the relation between the writers' language practices and political agendas. To begin a study of postmodern paratexts with the ghost of Maximus is an appropriate tribute, a reminder that many of these poets have a smaller audience not because their focus is self-consciously narrow but because they try to annex too much territory, to transform the very politics of language use. There are no isolated remarks in such a context; as Olson expressed it, one "cannot use any word / without using geography" (*Charles Olson in Mansfield* 16), geography in his sense of a communal space of landmark texts and mythic images to be analyzed. For Olson and subsequent American experimental poets, the relation between their poetry and paratexts at the very least has kept open the critical debates over how they engage that public space.

# 3

## *"Created to Explain": Jack Spicer's Exegetical Paratexts*

Jack Spicer concludes a mid-fifties letter to his friend Robin Blaser with
a half-serious curse for "any professor who reads this to his class from my *Col-
lected Letters*" ("Letters" 47).[1] Spicer, who with Blaser and Robert Duncan had
formed their own "Berkeley Renaissance" in the postwar Bay Area literary scene,
was just beginning at this time to explore new stylistic directions beyond his early
lyrics. Though only a few other poets and editors had read his writing, his let-
ters during the period convey a characteristic mix of ambition, self-doubt, and
humorous hostility about a poet's texts as public documents. Where Olson's para-
texts sprang from a desire to open communal boundaries and to contextualize
his poems for readers, it was Spicer's ambivalence toward public scrutiny that led
him to develop creative paratexts about receptive or menacing audiences.

What did a public or communal poetry signify for Spicer? His North Beach
*kreis,* modeled on Stefan George's circle of poets in Germany, was a group of
writers who shared his belief in language as an erotic, magical code that creates
its own priesthood. It was largely but not exclusively gay; in addition to Blaser
and to Duncan, who later distanced himself from Spicer, his circle of friends and
students at varying times included Joe Dunn, Helen Adam, George Stanley, John
Wieners, Stan Persky, and others, with occasional participation by a Beat poet
like Michael McClure, despite Spicer's general antagonism to the movement.
When Spicer gave a workshop on "Poetry as Magic" at the San Francisco Public
Library, his application questionnaire resembled an initiation rite, balancing
broad historical queries with practical concerns about which contemporary po-
ets the applicant would publish in a new literary magazine. Partly because he
restricted the publication of his own texts to Bay Area small presses like White
Rabbit, Spicer's writing never became as widely read as Olson's, yet he maintained
ties to experimental authors in Boston and New York and later to Vancouver lit-
erary circles.[2] Nor was he adverse to selective publicity; he mailed copies of his
1957 book *After Lorca* to canonical modernists (e.g., Eliot and Pound) as well as
to Olson and Ginsberg, whose relative popularity he both envied and satirized.[3]

In addition to these publications and to his own literary magazine *J,* Spicer
explored the idea of different popular forums for poetry while remaining deeply

skeptical about an audience's ability to appreciate his texts. In a 1949 symposium published by *Occident* magazine, he demanded that poets return to their cultural roots as "singers" and "entertainers" (*O* 92) before a "living audience" (91). He read and discussed his poems with friends at North Beach bars or parks, and he tried to translate that poetry scene for a wider audience as the setting of a detective novel begun in 1958. He nevertheless complains sardonically in *After Lorca* about the "fools that read these letters" (*CB* 15) and poetic dialogues. His Orpheus in a 1959 text rebukes an audience, "You have not listened to a word I have sung" (97). Even more frighteningly, when the listeners finally respond to the orphic singer with enthusiasm, they join the Maenads who murder him.

Spicer's hesitation about addressing a more mainstream audience is understandable. "[Y]ou can't get the individual politics, the politics you have as a poet, out of the national politics," he argued in a 1965 lecture at Berkeley (*L* 155). Like Olson's polis, Spicer's ideas of poetic community were shaped heavily by his McCarthy era experiences. His refusal to sign an anti-Communist loyalty oath as a linguistics graduate student at Berkeley had forced him to leave the university for two years. He was also writing during a period of increased political attacks on gays, police harassment, and dismissals of gay employees. Spicer believed, moreover, that poetry could not directly effect political change while the public could corrupt the poet. In the Berkeley lecture, he flatly stated that "most people will exploit poets" and advised his listeners that since they would all "sell out eventually," they should make sure that they at least obtained the best price for that decision (154).

Critics have described Spicer's writing as a confrontational dialogue between the poet and an outside community, and the complexity of that dialogue is reflected in the divided structures of his compositions.[4] Spicer juxtaposes disjunctive, minimalist poems with more accessible prose paratexts: creative prefaces, postscripts, commentaries, letters, manifestos, and mock textbooks. These paratexts allow him to stage carefully controlled performances of public exposure, instruction, and coy retreat in formats that he dismisses as inferior writing and yet concedes are essential to his poetry.

His paratextual narrators present themselves first as exegetes, a role with strong biblical connotations for Spicer. In "A Textbook of Poetry," he describes Christ as a Logos "created to Explain" His descent (*CB* 169) and then introduces his own commentary as something similarly "created to explain" (183) and disseminate a method of reading poetry. The exegete's problem is to prevent these extrapoetic explanations from becoming worldly or impure themselves, the Logos fallen to a "Lowghost" (178) in a prose whose slippery signifiers "miss what we hit" (167). Spicer's paratexts are full of taunts and injuries received in attempted communication, and his most extended prose foray into popular culture, the unfinished detective mystery, concerns the murder of an artist in which everyone in the neighborhood becomes a potential suspect.

Not surprisingly, many of Spicer's paratextual narrators shift between the persona of exegete and that of outlaw, dreaming of a mythical California frontier as a last retreat for poetic transgressors. "Let us fake out a frontier," the narrator entreats the audience in the opening prose section of *Billy the Kid,* "—a poem somebody could hide in with a sheriff's posse after him—a thousand miles of it if it is necessary for him to go a thousand miles" (*CB* 79). The feinting or fakery is the crucial term. Even as the paratexts offer to explain Spicer's poetics, their utopian communal element lies not in a specific outline for a new Pacific Republic of American poetry but in their misdirections, fake borderlands, half-maps, and half-truths in which literal-minded interpreters as well as the most versatile readers can lose their bearings. I trace the genesis of those misdirections from some of Spicer's earliest prose paratexts to books that integrate both poetry and commentary in their formats.

## Unverting a Community: Spicer's Manifestos

Spicer's paratexts of the fifties already reflect an uneasiness with the Romantic idea of the poet as communal prophet. "Some Notes on Whitman for Allen Joyce," a prose commentary that Spicer would include with a selection of early poems for Donald Allen, depicts the American Kosmos as an unrequited lover "whose fine mouth has sucked the cock of the heart of the country for fifty years" (*O* 81). The blunt description disrupts what Spicer punningly calls Whitman's "fairy story" (82), a fantasy of gay camaraderie as a model for national community. "Calamus is like Oz," the narrator complains, because "You did not ever understand cruelty. It was that that severed your world from me. . . The comrade you are walking with suddenly twists your hand off" (81), certainly an impediment to future poetry writing. Spicer correlates the knowledge of that cruelty with biblical images of the fall from a "lost paradise" to contemplate "your damned Calamus" (82) with nothing but "the ghost of something crucified" as a role model for the word-giver's relation to an audience (81).

Spicer creates his own anti-*Calamus* using European avant-garde models in his 1956 prose sequence lengthily entitled "The Unvert Manifesto and Other Papers Found in the Rare Book Room of the Boston Public Library in the Handwriting of Oliver Charming. By S." This mock manifesto, its setting a memento of Spicer's brief employment in the Boston Public Library, pays homage to the Dada manifestos that Spicer had been reading in Robert Motherwell's anthology—Kurt Schwitters's descriptions of his Merz art or Tristan Tzara's paragraphs of provocations, contradictions and antitheorizing.[5] Spicer borrows not only the absurdist language of post–World War I Dada but also the artists' heightened sense of distance from the states they imagined, their humorously grand visions of international artistic communes registering a disillusionment with national politics. Spicer's narrative jumps from the most general to the most specific contexts, analyzing "'Western civilization'" in the same sentence as the crowd at "'the bar last night'" as it ponders whether the extravagant rhetoric of "'Dada and Mertz'" revolutionizing human sexual relations simply reflects the isolation of the unsuccessful artist (*CB* 344).

If the primary function of a manifesto, moreover, is to call public attention to the movement and the artists, then Spicer's text at first seems to be the signature of a communal unvert or introvert indeed. The author is reduced to a single letter and presented through the pseudonymous "handwriting" of Oliver Charming, purportedly S.'s fellow writer. Instead of telling us much about S., Charming appends to the manifesto a diary of his own sexual and literary exploits, yet here too the references are more wistful than self-promoting: "'No angel as yet. I wonder if I could steal one'" (*CB* 345). The strongest statement of poetic influence on politics is Charming's suspicion: "'Something is going on between S. and history'" (342)—most likely, he implies, something lewdly digressive and un-printable. Hints that the best action is happening offstage create the impression of a text simultaneously addressed to two different audiences, a group of insiders privy to the characters' charades and the spectators who never entirely catch all the references.

The manifesto argues, however, that it is not always possible for a writer to separate those two audiences, if only because mainstream America has already co-opted so much of the avant-gardist's territory. Where Schwitters incorporated street debris into his art, the local street scenes seem to swallow up the artist in Spicer's manifesto. One of the characters, Sidney Mertz, presumably a founder of the Unvert movement, is a well-reformed Futurist previously "arrested for drunken driving of a steam locomotive" but now established as "the bartender of the American Legion bar in Jackson, Wyoming" (*CB* 341). As S. himself assesses the unvert's chances for rebellion, "'We homosexuals are the only minority group that completely lacks any vestige of a separate cultural heritage. We have no songs, no folklore, even our customs are borrowed from our upper-middleclass mothers'" (344). It is an appropriately ironic twist that this manifesto with its subversive commands to "masturbate on street corners" (341) becomes a "Found" object in a roomful of famous books as if the canon itself were a textual collage that could subsume oppositional pieces within its framework. Even the copyist's last name, Charming, recalls one of Tzara's favorite adjectives in his manifestos, "charmant"; Tzara used the term partly in self-mockery but also to suggest an audience's ability to turn a disruptive performance into an amusingly quaint spectacle.[6]

As Spicer negotiates between a marginal poetic community and a mainstream cultural heritage, he develops writing strategies in "The Unvert Manifesto" that anticipate the techniques of his later books.[7] The manifesto narrator creates a "MERTZ" language of "Nonsense" (*CB* 341), of negations, repetitions, and circular definitions, as a playful barrier between himself and the reader: "An unvert is neither an invert or an outvert, a pervert or a convert, an introvert or a retrovert" (341). As in the Dada texts, nonsense as something against or in excess of communicative meaning—with the pun on Mertz/merde as waste—pokes fun at the manifesto as a political document. Yet the games and the multiple personae are also designed to intensify reader curiosity, a ploy that the manifesto suggests when it refers to nonsense as "an act of friendship" (341), an act more often figured erotically in the text's obsessive sexual pursuits. "'I must unvent someone named Graham Macarel,'" Charming asserts in his diary. "'He should be about seventeen or eighteen and have a large Dada. I can use him as the hero and victim of my Mertzcycle . . .'" (342, author's ellipsis), adding in a subsequent description, "'(Note—I must be sure to call him Mac. Graham reminds the uninformed imagination of crackers.)'" (342). The humorous sound play and antilyrical style interrupt the tension of a romance with an idealized reader, modeled on Spicer's student Graham Mackintosh, who nevertheless fails to fully understand his teacher. "''Why did you have to invent Graham Macarel?''" S. asks Charming (343) and then continues, "''Why didn't you invent syphilis instead''" (343), a complaint that parallels love with communication as infection. Charming deflects that infectious contact by framing Macarel as a fictional disciple whose seductiveness can be created and de-created as "Dada" jokes. The diary concludes with an interrupted climax, "'I am gradually able to have the most Mertzian sexual'" (345)—a fragment that tantalizes the reader while leaving the imagination "uninformed."

Spicer would return to the parodic manifesto form to explore different images of the gay artist in a later piece like "Three Marxist Essays," a sixties text that alternately defines homosexuality as "being alone" (*O* 88) and imagines an avant-garde debauched by outsiders who want to participate in the movement: "If we let our love flower into the true revolution we will be swamped with offers for beds" (88). More frequently, however, Spicer incorporates his paratexts about a public avant-garde art within the poetry texts themselves, contrasting their different styles of audience address and literary allusion.

## "Because These Letters Are Unnecessary": *After Lorca*

Following "The Unvert Manifesto," Spicer's 1957 translation text *After Lorca* marks a critical transition in his articulation of a communal poetics. He was fascinated by Federico García Lorca's deep image poetry and his biography, not least because the Spanish poet's death seemed to embody Spicer's worst fears about public persecution. Lorca was murdered in 1936 by Falangist troops as a leftist sympathizer; his homosexuality may also have helped to make him a target. Spicer's response to that violence is a tribute book structured by two sets of text-paratext dialogues that link Lorca to Spicer's *kreis* of poets: the Lorca lyrics that Spicer translates (and invents) and then a series of flirtatious prose letters to Lorca that expound Spicer's poetic translation theory.

Ostensibly, the act of translation already presupposes a belief that meaning can be shared across different cultural contexts. In its letters and creative additions to Lorca's poems, Spicer's book transplants the poet's Granada to North Beach scenes that are decades distant and claims to have resurrected the original author in the process. "Lorca" takes an active part in the book's conversation, writing a preface to the volume and offering a few new poems "written after my death" (*CB* 11), presumably some of the eleven original poems that Spicer mixes in the translations as he plays ghost-writer to his hero. The fiction of Lorca's presence serves two roles. It places Spicer's own writing in an established experimental tradition, and it asserts the power of his contemporary *kreis* against a government that murdered one of their predecessors. To make the community more tangible, he dedicates most of the translations in the volume to individual writer friends as if extending Lorca's influence to their own projects.

The book's two sets of text-paratext relations—the translated source lyrics and the prose letters that gloss these poems—must be read against each other, not only because the two sequences are juxtaposed throughout *After Lorca* but also because Spicer's translation theory is based initially on a generic distinction between poetry and prose that gradually breaks down in the book's dialogues. "Prose invents—poetry discloses," he writes in the first letter, relegating "weak" prose (*CB* 15) to a superfluous or fictitious communication while poetry conveys its objects with terse precision. His theory of translation as a correspondence rather than a connection (34) depends on a poetic economy in which a modern author's creative language games respond to a previous poet's texts without any wasted words of explication: "[Tradition] means generations of different poets in different countries patiently telling the same story, writing the same poem, gaining and losing something with each transformation—but, of course, never really losing anything" (15). While the specific incident described or the poetic form may change, poetry's ability to "disclose" experience is still preserved in each new text. He informs Lorca in the second letter:

> When I translate one of your poems and I come across words I
> do not understand, I always guess at their meanings. I am inevita-
> bly right. A really perfect poem (no one yet has written one) could

be perfectly translated by a person who did not know one word of the language it was written in. A really perfect poem has an infinitely small vocabulary. (25)

The ideal translation might not deal in reified language at all but would be a direct intuitive transference of "the immediate object, the immediate emotion" (25) from writer to writer as if both were corresponding in a Baudelairean landscape where one sensation blurs imperceptibly into another. Choosing Lorca with his images of mirrors, pools, and gazing Narcissus figures heightens the effect of one kindred spirit mirroring the other in closeted communication.

In practice, however, Spicer's refusal to indicate which of the poems are translations, which his own lyrics, and which a combination of the two has the opposite effect. Instead of suggesting the correspondence between paratextual source and translation, it provokes the reader to find out exactly what has been lost or added in Spicer's version. Apart from the new Spicer poems, there are phrases, lines, and even stanzas that are altered from the original Spanish, which is not included in this text. While many of the poems correspond roughly to the sense of their source paratexts, a few, as Clayton Eshleman points out, are changed so substantially that it is difficult to recognize the original. The translations themselves range from texts like the angry, provocative "Ode for Walt Whitman" that stand on their own as English poems to stilted renditions that call attention to their own awkwardness. While Spicer is not the only poet to discuss a translation based on characteristics other than semantics, the vagueness about criteria for textual correspondences combined with the doctrine of the translator's infallibility may make the reader question how far the poetic exchange with Lorca goes beyond Spicer's private language games.

The prose preface and letters, the book's literal correspondence, reveal that Spicer's unusual translation project stems from deeper concerns over the dissemination and interpretation of a poem even when the audience is limited to other writers. In many poetic tributes to a predecessor, for example, the older author seems wholly absorbed by the modern; one thinks of Olson and Melville or Howe and Dickinson. The "Lorca" in Spicer's preface, in contrast, is polite but "unsympathetic" to versions of his poems that he disavows as translations and declares the "waste of a considerable talent" (*CB* 11). He does not clarify that the talent is Spicer's.

This cagey "Lorca" mirrors Spicer's fears about the reception of his own poetry. Although the translations may be dedicated to friends, Spicer's persona grumbles in the letters that there are only two friends who know how to read his work, few peers who approve of it, and a crowd of younger writers trying to copy his ideas. He worries that his texts will be exposed to potential scoffers without his consent. The distinction between a private poetry and prosy public conversations breaks down in his half-humorous, half-nightmarish letter fantasies of a poem as a promiscuous independent agent that will "demand imperiously that you share it with somebody" (*CB* 38) or simply go off with the first purchaser:

> Some poems are easily laid. They will give themselves to anybody and anybody physically capable can receive them. . . . I swear that if one of them were hidden beneath my carpet, it would shout out and seduce somebody. (38)

These poems can transform the most private domestic space into a brothel. The image of wanton lyrics as lurking figures in the carpet is particularly invasive, since Spicer in one of his invented "Lorca" poems describes the writer's voice as a dictation machine caught in the body's "big, dark carpets" (46). Putting the two images together, a poem's demand for readers to appreciate it metaphorically makes the artist's body seem equally exposed to strangers, as if the poem were prompting him to invite his own violation. Even "quiet" poems, Spicer adds in his letter, are simply waiting to "be seduced" with no guarantee that they will be "properly wed" in the end (38). Given these choices, the purist's desire to find a "really perfect poem" (25) to translate seems unlikely to be fulfilled.

Instead, the letters betray an increasing fascination with the role of exegetical prose in the process of translation. The first letter, for all its condemnations of prose as the weak excesses of everyday vocabulary, a genre associated with images of crowds, crime, excrement, and madness, also justifies Spicer's correspondence with Lorca as a means of clearing away verbal refuse before the poetry can be translated:

> These letters are to be as temporary as our poetry is to be permanent. They will establish the bulk, the wastage that my sour-stomached contemporaries demand to help them swallow and digest the pure word. We will use up our rhetoric here so that it will not appear in our poems. Let it be consumed paragraph by paragraph, day by day, until nothing of it is left in our poetry and nothing of our poetry is left in it. It is precisely because these letters are unnecessary that they must be written. (*CB* 15)

The biblical vehemence of this diatribe against prose is belied by the fact that Spicer keeps writing the letters to Lorca. The last sentence in the quoted excerpt makes the point clearly: these prose passages are vital precisely because they are an unnecessary or imperfect communication. Like the verbal play in "The Unvert Manifesto," their gossipy tone, colloquialisms, and clichés break up the intensity of the poetic project, distancing the speaker not only from a seductive predecessor but also from the readers that Spicer continues to court and who indeed demand the prose discussions in order to properly "digest" his work. When he imagines having a barroom discussion of poetics, Spicer's persona reassures himself in the opening letter that "nothing will happen because we will be speaking in prose" (15). "It was a game, I shout to myself. A game," he concludes about his translation project in the last letter, making sure that the influence of correspondent or reader, however "contagious" it seems, remains "disembodied" and unable to harm him (51).

The more closely one scrutinizes his poetic dialogue with Lorca, the more one realizes the importance of the themes and stylistic techniques that Spicer first associates with prose, for he begins to incorporate some of the devices at strategic points in the poetic translations themselves. He uses a flat, colloquial, repetitive style of satire at intervals to mediate the "Terrible Presence" (*CB* 36) of the outsiders who attract and threaten Lorca's narrators; Spicer turns the poet's vulnerability into bathos.[8] When the sounds of mourning invade the poet's room, for example, in "The Ballad of Weeping," Spicer deflates that intrusive grief by translating the Spanish "inmenso" (Lorca 172) repeatedly as "big": "But the weeping is a big dog / The weeping is a big angel / The weeping is a big violin" (*CB* 26). Such deliberately clumsy passages throw the readers off balance as well, forcing them to negotiate tonal shifts between source and translation, between one translated lyric and the next, and often between sections within the same translation. Understanding the ironic remarks, as Burton Hatlen notes, allows the reader to join the poet's community of knowing insiders (122), and yet the subtle gradations of Spicer's satire in the Lorca dialogues make that sense of membership unstable. One keeps double checking texts and paratexts for the right cue to smile.

The "translation" that provides one of Spicer's most detailed models for wooing readers at arm's length in *After Lorca* is written as a drama in poetic prose. An original piece that Spicer attributes to Lorca, "Buster Keaton Rides Again: A Sequel" tests out different representations of the relation between artist and audience. It opens with an image of failed translation as Spicer's Keaton carries a dictionary in his pocket but is unable to interpret his audience's language: "I don't understand what anybody is talking about" (*CB* 42). Carrying over the images of waste and madness that Spicer connects with prose, literary critics disguised as chambermaids attend Keaton's performance, as the actor tells spectators attracted by the public posturing of the Beats that he is "not going to Rockland" with them (43). Engaging an audience or discussing an idealized community does not merely make the writer vulnerable on this stage; the declaration "I announce a new world" is tantamount to saying "I announce the death of Orpheus"

(44), the poet dismembered by a crowd of frustrated seducers. Spicer's Keaton preempts that threat with his own campy poses, offering himself as a martyr for universal love through exaggerated clichés: dangling by his heels from a crucifix, distributing rosaries to policemen, and displaying his bleeding heart as he chants, "I love you. I love you. . . . No kidding, I love you" for the spectators' benefit (44). Spicer gives the audience parts in the play, transforming them into stock characters through melodramatic stage directions about the critics as villains who bring down the curtain or the anonymous fan who indiscriminately kisses all the characters "Suddenly, at the last possible time before the curtain falls" (44). The point of such carefully scripted encounters, Spicer suggests in a letter, is to anticipate and "encys[t] the intruder" (48) within the poet's own compositional framework.

As Spicer's persona in *After Lorca* moves from a theory of the perfect poem to experiments with framing devices of "explanations," "promise[s]," and "warning[s]" (*CB* 51), he concedes that some prosaic instructions for the reader may be a necessary part of the poetic process. Looking back at the book's text-paratext juxtapositions from the preface, "Lorca" explains that the chatty prose letters signed "Love, Jack" are staged for the benefit of an outside audience:

> When Mr. Spicer began sending them to me a few months ago, I
> recognized immediately the "programmatic letter"—the letter one
> poet writes to another not in any effort to communicate with him,
> but rather as a young man whispers his secrets to a scarecrow, know-
> ing that his young lady is in the distance listening. The young lady
> in this case may be a Muse, but the scarecrow nevertheless quite na-
> turally resents the confidences. The reader, who is not a party to this
> singular tryst, may be amused by what he overhears. (*CB* 11–12)

One talks to a predecessor, the passage asserts, in a competitive correspondence that reduces the other author to a straw man. Yet even so, the "dead are notoriously hard to satisfy" (12), whereas "Lorca" suggests that the living reader who stumbles upon the tryst would be more intrigued by the indirect, voyeuristic presentation of craft secrets in Spicer's prose. Although "Lorca" may be ambivalent about the need to please a "contemporary audience" (12), he nevertheless places the reader in a similar eavesdropping position in the love triangle as the beloved/Muse whose approval the poet requires.

Spicer directly associates his Muse with public exposure through exegetical prose in a letter to a friend included in his next poem series, a 1958 text suggestively entitled *Admonitions*. The letter offers a compromise in the debates over the role of poetry and paratexts in *After Lorca:*

Dear Joe,

> Some time ago I would have thought that writing notes on par-
> ticular poems would either be a confession that the poems were to-
> tally inadequate (a sort of a patch put on a leaky tire) or an equally
> humiliating confession that the writer was more interested in the
> terrestrial mechanics of criticism than the celestial mechanics of
> poetry—in either case that the effort belonged to the garage or stable
> rather than to the Muse.
>
> Muses do exist, but now I know that they are not afraid to dirty
> their hands with explication—that they are patient with truth and
> commentary as long as it doesn't get into the poem, that they whis-
> per (if you let yourself really hear them), "Talk all you want, baby,
> but *then* let's go to bed." (*CB* 55)

The passage still makes the distinction between celestial poetry and fallen com-
mentary-as-waste. Blending the two is a "dirtying" operation that threatens to
transform the Muses into street corner pickups like the whorish poems in *After
Lorca* that make themselves too available to readers. The poet is reduced to con-
fessing his inadequacies and sins rather than instructing disciples. But the erotic
pleasure here is at least refocused on the poet, with the prose explication becoming
the foreplay that gives the author access to his creative inspiration. The narra-
tors in Spicer's most extensive paratextual book explore the implications of this
exegetical foreplay at length as they attempt to craft more ambitious narratives
of a poetic community.

## Poetry and Its Afterwords

Spicer's *The Heads of the Town Up to the Aether,* published in 1962, employs a
variety of paratexts to explain its poetic techniques. The book has three sections:
the first a group of poems complemented by prose explanatory notes, the second
a "Fake Novel" in paragraph form with two inserted lyrics, and the third a prose
composition entitled "A Textbook of Poetry." Since Spicer models the three sec-
tions loosely on Dante's *Divine Comedy,* the progress toward paradise involves more
and more space devoted to paratextual prose. The reason for the shift toward
paratexts is not only the recognized need for readerly exegesis but also, paradoxi-
cally, the narrators' growing awareness of the limitations of that explication.

The first section, "Homage to Creeley," was originally published as a set of
poems to which the notes were later added (Foster 35). The page layout of the
final text heightens the initial distinction in *After Lorca* between minimalist
poetry and exegetical correspondence. Each page is divided in half by a dark

line across the middle, the upper portion consisting of a short poem while the conversational explanatory note below is set in lighter type like an inferior echo of the lines above, a liminal gray space where the text addresses readers more directly.

There is no poetry on the first page, only a title and dedications (see fig. 3.1). The substitution of homages for poems on this page and particularly the reference to Cégeste, the dead poet who speaks to the living author via car radio in Jean Cocteau's 1950 film version of *Orphée,* seem to support critics' claims that this is one of Spicer's most orphic books "dictated" by multiple outside sources.[9] "Homage" alone engages Shakespeare, Dante, Poe, Emerson, Crane, Carroll, and other authors, as well as the white noise of local broadcasts, bar jokes, and pickup lines. What is most significant, however, in the two opening dedications, is that the sources suggest variations on the Lorca/Orpheus figure as a warning about the multiple dangers a poet faces from his audience. In the Cocteau storyline, Orphée is a former avant-gardist who is now too much the public celebrity to produce any genuinely new poetry, nor does that celebrity prevent his eventual murder. The dedication to Creeley, in turn, recalls the Black Mountain poet's fractured lyrics of betrayal and violence in *The Charm* or the early poems of *For Love,* where friends and lovers readily join sides with the poet's public enemies. Spicer's "Homage" creates an even darker American cityscape of junkies, soldiers, bordello customers, and vicious lovers who target the poet.

The lower commentary suggests a different narrative approach to the city. Unlike the poet, the commentator is vividly present on the first page, bragging about his ability to seduce "all of the people in the poems" (*CB* 117) where the poet has failed. The exegete can make those public seductions by posing as "the ghost of answering questions" (117). Building on the manifestos and the overheard letters in *After Lorca,* Spicer makes the notes an ongoing tease that promises directions but never fully clarifies the lyrics above it. "Beware me. Keep me at a distance as I keep you at a distance," he warns us (117), at the same time that the notes take the confidential tone of someone with juicy inside details on a hitherto exclusive movement.

While Spicer theoretically advocates a dictated poetry of radical openness to outside sources, he uses the lyrics and notes in "Homage to Creeley" to stage two different strategies for mediating intrusions from hostile or ignorant readers. The lyrics generate images of enclosure with their references to gates, arks, pails, and blankets. The nursery rhyme formats recall the nonsense sound games of "The Unvert Manifesto," but instead of the manifesto's hints of secret encounters with a thinly disguised student, this speaker records a series of losses in a poème à clef whose terse lines more carefully conceal the characters' identities:

# Homage to Creeley

## Explanatory Notes

I

For Cegeste

To begin with, I could have slept with all of the people in the poems. It is not as difficult as the poet makes it. That is the reason I was born tonight.

He wanted an English professor—someone he could feel superior to, as a ghost. He wanted to eliminate all traces of the poetry. To kiss someone goodbye but you people out there know none of the answers either—even the simple questions the poet was asked.

I am the ghost of answering questions. Beware me. Keep me at a distance as I keep you at a distance.

Cegeste died at the age of nineteen. Just between the time when one could use one's age as a power and one uses one's age as a crutch. (cf. A Fake Novel About the Life of Arthur Rimbaud). At 35 one throws away crutches. (cf. Inferno Canto I)

Two loves I had. One rang a bell
Connected on both sides with hell

The other'd written me a letter
In which he said I've written better

They pushed their cocks in many places
And I'm not certain of their faces
Or which I kissed or which I didn't
Or which of both of them I hadn't.

(CB 118)

If the poet does not quite "eliminate all traces of the poetry" (117), as the exegete says he wants to, this lyric erases the names and blurs the features of the unkind lovers, at least one of whom is also the poet's reader. The short tetrameter lines in rhyming couplets and the pun on belles lettres help to create a sense of formal closure against the threatening review, which is equated here with the aggressive "cocks" that had penetrated the poet's body. The one correspondence that a prying "English professor" (117) would clearly catch, the parody of Shakespeare's sonnet 144, neatly turns the criticism that the poet has "written better" into a hint that the ex-lover/reader may have underestimated another Bard.

In his most ambitious "Homage" lyrics, the poet dreams of extending a protective enclosure to the entire *kreis,* promising that "Our history / It stays / In a closet we wear like a ring on our fingers" (*CB* 136), a mixed trope in which the shared history of a gay poets' circle becomes a symbolic marriage pledge among participants to conceal that past. But histories are hard to read in a dark closet, nor can an enclosed place remain secret if it is openly displayed as a sign of membership. Like the ring that advertises what should be concealed, the explanatory notes in "Homage" are a constant reminder of the poet's failure to isolate the poem from outside readers. These prose paratexts adopt a different technique to shape reader response.

The notes work by excessive instructions that ultimately frustrate meaningful interpretation. The exegete coaxes pushy readers who "want to be sure of themselves" (*CB* 118), insisting that he alone has the right directions. "The singer and the song are something The Poet did (does) not understand" (131), he sighs, while "you people out there know none of the answers either—even the simple questions the poet was asked" (117). Compared with the lyrics' brief vignettes, the notes do provide some narrative progression for the Cocteau references (e.g., "Orpheus and Eurydice are in their last nuptial embrace during this poem" [122]), while declaring the importance of their advice in dramatic asides: "This is definitely a warning to Orpheus" (127). But the right directions give the wrong conclusions here; the attempt to map out poetic formats or to cordon off a communal history, the exegete suggests, leads only to a loss of clear boundaries. "Tragedy has exact limits," he explains, but they are limits "that Hell cannot enclose" (135), no matter how epigrammatically the poet defines his past.

The notes instead identify patterns of images so generalized that they offer the reader little guidance: "If you watch closely you will see that water appears and disappears in the poem" (*CB* 120). The explanations at their most sarcastic are obvious or redundant ("Actually, L.A. is Los Angeles" [119]), the adverbs "actually," "really," and "naturally" parodying claims of truth-value as the paratexts refer us back to simulacra: "there was a motion picture that showed everything" (119). The best commentary "show[s] everything" and tells nothing, its play drawing out the sheer amount of conflicting textual information to be interpreted. It's "too bad" that Orpheus—and, by implication, the reader—misunderstood the purpose of the underworldly directions, the exegete remarks, "because there would have been just as much poetry if he had understood it" (127).

In deferring interpretive closure, these explanatory notes serve a similar function as Olson's parenthetical asides to the reader, yet the model of community is very different.[10] Where Olson saw a polis whose borders would be flexible enough to include multiple textual formulations of citizenship, Spicer shows writers whose texts are elided or changed in "Civil War[s]" (*CB* 141) over literary and political influence. When quarrelsome predecessors, for example, try to get the poet's attention, they elect a representative who is "almost a Congresswoman for them" (128), the "almost" implying that their messages inevitably will be distorted. Spicer's exegete boasts openly about his literary annexations, changing Emerson's "Concord Hymn" for Revolutionary War soldiers into the discordant sexual boast "'Conquered Him'" (120), a reading that gives new meaning to the original poem's raised shaft and the fired shot heard around the world. But any revolutionary conquest in this infernal America is also impermanent, and the exegete finds car wrecks and guard stations in his path when he tries to project his own vision of a Pacific Republic onto the country as a whole. "Fort Wayne," he writes, the Indiana home of one of Spicer's protégés, James Alexander, "stands on the American fortress between California and reality" (140), a remark that transforms California into an illusory refuge for artists that can be re-created only in isolated armed camps in the rest of the nation.

While "Homage"'s parodic definitions and dangerous, shifting borders do not lend themselves easily to utopian models, they call attention to the limitations of any one poetic style or definition of a poets' community. This dilemma begins to suggest the role of the purgatory section of *The Heads of the Town*, a prose composition with the title "A Fake Novel About the Life of Arthur Rimbaud."

What is a fake novel, a fictional fiction of a poet's life? Spicer not only Americanizes the French avant-gardist by interweaving his story with events from United States political history but also distorts or invents biographical facts in chapters with eye-catching titles like "Back To His Genitals" (*CB* 165), "An Embarrassing Folksong" (158), and "Rimbaud Is A Gorilla With Seven Teeth" (160). Beneath the surreal tabloid headlines, this novel is both a tribute to Rimbaud's experiments in prose poetry and a whodunit mystery. By foregrounding the fictiveness of the biography genre, the novelist tries to move beyond clichés of the alienated avant-gardist to figure out who really "stole the signs" of the author's "youth and his poetry" (164), turning him away from his art.

The story of Rimbaud as a young gay prodigy who defies literary and social conventions and then renounces poetry forever at age twenty seems custom-made for Spicer's investigative portrait of the avant-gardist. One of the text's two poetic chapters satirizes the myth of an *enfant terrible* who repeatedly threatens to "leave the stage / And bite off all my toes" (*CB* 153). In looking at Rimbaud's career, the novelist does not absolve readers who might have been oblivious to the "dreamings of poets" (161), but he also tacitly suggests the French poet as a "fake" or disengaged life, an artist caught in Spicer's familiar quandary between an ideal concept of poetry and the need to respond to a specific historical community. The novelist imaginatively recasts the young Rimbaud both as a purist who "could not imagine persons to listen to the new language" he invents (151) and an impressionable performer who sings everyone's blues in the middle of a bar.

Rimbaud's later years are still more problematic for the novelist. Even if poetry makes nothing happen, Spicer's orphic Rimbaud becomes another kind of "dead-letter officer" (*CB* 164) when he gives up art only to contribute to the materialism and provincial prejudice he had denounced. In a wonderfully layered critique, the novelist describes Rimbaud shooting at the white and black race horses from Plato's discussion of love in the *Phaedrus,* the pun on race evoking the young poet's exotic images of dark-skinned savages in his writing as well as Rimbaud's subsequent career as an African gun-runner and possibly a slave trader. "To love," the novelist states, "is not to continue with the Zanzibar slave trade. To continue with the Zanzibar slave trade is not to love" (*CB* 152). The shifting slave references blur into allusions to the American Civil War and to more recent battlefields as the text rehearses "the old content of war": "We were not human, the others were not human" (155). The novelist implicitly questions what "real addresses" (162) to an audience, whether poetic or exegetical narratives, might move readers beyond a discourse of dehumanized subjects.

Discussions of human cities and divine love dominate the book's third section, the prose passages in "A Textbook of Poetry." If Rimbaud is the predecessor who "fails us whenever we have a nerve to need him" (*CB* 164), "A Textbook" explores more fully the ways that a failed exegesis can show readers something beyond its own limitations. Despite its urgent efforts to "Teach" (*CB* 170) and "explain" (180), the textbook offers no formulaic instructions about reading but rather a succession of metaphors for poetry: a stage performance, an awkward prayer, an unfinished jigsaw puzzle. In developing these metaphors, the exegete elides the distinction between real objects and artistic illusions. Defining what Spicer means by the "real" in his poetry is already difficult, as Lori Chamberlain observes, because his use of the term seems to oscillate between Platonic forms and Aristotelian objects in flux (432–33). In "A Textbook," artifice reshapes reality. Surrealism becomes an "imaginary" kingdom that issues real stamps (*CB* 180); a magician's rope ladder "Descends to the real" (172) at the moment when its suspension is revealed as a "trick" (173).

The descriptive confusion over real objects is appropriate, the exegete emphasizes, since the "real" is more than what is humanly perceptible or expressible. "The real poetry" is something "beyond us": "Christ, the Logos unbelieved in" because we have a "habit of seeing" only the most familiar scenes and communicative patterns (*CB* 183). A textbook "created to explain" its own limitations as a "fake" (183) is the first step toward recognizing a "vesicle of truth" that is "Extended past what the words mean and below, God damn it, what the words are" (182), as the gaps and contradictions of a fallen poetic language evoke by contrast the unity of the original Logos.[11] "A Textbook" stops symbolically at section 29, for the twenty-ninth canto in Dante's *Paradiso* is the last one before the ascent to the heavenly Empyrean. Beatrice in this canto denounces preachers who pass off their own interpretations as scriptural truth. Spicer's text, in contrast, asks readers to imagine something "more than the words" (*CB* 183) of a speaker "wanting to explain" (180), in both senses of *wanting* as desiring and lacking. By making Augustine's distinction between using an imperfect temporal resource as a means to an end rather than enjoying it for its own sake, Spicer partly erases the stigma of wasteful exegesis that haunts his paratexts.

Spicer's linguistic leap of faith in this section is also a vision of community. "The city redefined becomes a church," he asserts, a church organized as a "movement of poetry" by *kreis*-like participants (*CB* 176). The "temple," predictably, is set out "in the weeds and California wildflowers" where "we worship words" (175); the contemporary West Coast cityscapes he describes anticipate the divine city "in an utterly mixed and mirrored way" (176). The correspondence takes place through the current inhabitants' shared sense of loss and displacement rather than a unifying presence. "Every city that is formed collects its slums," the exegete writes, and "its ghosts" (175). Every resident experiences alienation in looking at "the scattered nature" of what he or she now perceives as "reality" (176) while trying, as the speaker does, to picture a community of both "beliefs" and "hearts," a city, he confesses, "that I do not remember" (176). This lost past that is also a future utopia offers a spiritual version of the American revolutionary tradition that continually needs to be rediscovered. Spicer transforms the image from *Billy the Kid* of "fak[ing] out a frontier" where poetic outlaws can hide (79) into the description of a community where each citizen is an exiled rebel seeking to return home with nothing but fake maps for guides.

Acknowledging a common exile does not eliminate the fierce conflicts within the temporal city, the jockeying over who gets to write the local history of a poetry movement or the national narratives of good citizens and sinister strangers. The exegete still snipes at the audience that a "human love object is untrue. / Screw you" (*CB* 177). Nevertheless, he insists, "We do not hate the human beings that listen to [a textbook of poetry], read it, make comments on it" (183). Poetic magic, in his often-cited metaphor of the Indian rope trick, is no longer arcane knowledge that the writer offers to select initiates but a deconstructive act in which the performer reveals his sleight of hand to the whole audience. That audience can either respond as textbook-loving academics who "leave satisfied" in "Knowing how the trick was played" (173), or they can appreciate the performance as something more than the fragmented stages of its explication.

There is a third possibility in the audience scenario, the chance that members might respond to the poetic performance with tricks of their own. If words are treacherous tools falling short of the Logos, the exegete declares, then it is "up to us to astonish them and Him" (*CB* 178), to find the right word play as "pathology" that "leads to new paths and pathfinding" (179). When the exegete challenges "A Textbook"'s readers to "Imagine" its sentences "as lyric poetry" (177) or when the novelist warns that the reader will become "Involved in the lives" of a poet as fictional subject (167), they dare the audience to compose an *After Spicer,* to "mess around," to "totally destroy the pieces" the author sets up, or at least to "build around them" (176) a different version of the redeemed city.

It is a remarkable invitation that a number of writers have taken up directly or indirectly. There is Robin Blaser's creative afterword to the *Collected Books,* his essay title, "The Practice of Outside" (269), recalling the ghostly signature of Spicer's Lorca writing posthumously from "Outside Granada" where he was killed (12). Blaser charts a "continuing recognition" (326) of Spicer's poetic arguments that still resonate within and outside the *kreis,* and he also acknowledges any commentary as an infernal distortion of Spicer's words. "I am here entering that combat for language which was Jack's," he announces. "And I'm having a hell of a time with the description of the process which he performed. I feel my language thicken and become more abstract" (291). Instead of a conventional analysis, he reproduces Spicer's creative process by presenting another set of shifting exegetical clues that thicken the plot, or one plot, of Spicer's corpse/corpus as a "detective story" (287) in which the author's assassin is revealed as his own commitment to an orphic poetry: *"My vocabulary did this to me"* (325).

Stephen Jonas, the Boston poet to whom Spicer dedicated his translation of Lorca's ode to Whitman, created a number of tribute pieces to Spicer compositions. "Cante Jondo" gives a flamenco twist to Spicer's own homages to Lorca and "Bird," with a playful nod to the readerly asides of "Soul Brother Jack" (160): "Jack Spicer says wait, don't leave, the poem's not over yet" (162) in his quest to "save America from / the abuses of rime" (160). Spicer as angry mentor in Jonas's poem finally seems to have bridged the gap from coast to coast, and yet, in a telling metaphor, Jonas's crusader gets national attention only as the object of a paranoid plot of enclosure: "All over America the little magazines conspired / to board Jack Spicer up in a California Street rooming house, / for lack of space" (163). The reader is left to wonder whether the avant-gardists on the editorial boards are ignoring Spicer or listening too closely, reflecting back the ambivalence about exposing one's poetry to public criticism that colors even his insistent paratextual demands for reader response.

Spicer's own "Textbook of Poetry" stands as a series of visionary moments that already anticipate their dissolution. Playing with the "Aether" in the book's title, the exegete looks ahead to the point "when the gas explodes" and "the ghosts disappear," holy or unholy, leaving the author back with a "city of chittering human beings" (*CB* 178). Spicer never fully resolved what he expected from that quotidian audience. After *The Heads of the Town,* there are few books with discrete sections of prose commentary that scrutinizes its own indirection or insufficiency. Several of Spicer's narrators suggest that explicating paratexts may indeed be excessive in light of readers' preference for less complicated messages and delivery. "For you I would build a whole new universe," the poet tells a bored listener in *Language,* "but you obviously find it cheaper to rent one" (229) that is already familiar. *The Holy Grail,* Spicer's first book after *The Heads of the Town,* does rely on conventional forms like the monologue and on the well-known plots of Arthurian legends, while his last two books range from allusive word games to more transparent forms of political protest against the events of "Western Imperialism" (264), critiques whose sentences can seem stripped of his earlier satiric complexity:

They've (the leaders of our country) have become involved in a
    network of lies.
We (the poets) have also become in network of lies by opposing
    them.

. . . . . . . . . . . . . . . . . . . . . . . . . . . . . . . . . . . .
What is important is what we don't kill each other with
And a loving hand reaches a loving hand.

(*CB* 267)

His images of corpses in Hiroshima and Vietnam threaten to become the "corpse of an image" (220), a frozen description of territories under siege that cannot be transformed by the poet's parodic alchemy—the antithesis of Maximus's American dream of causal mythologies.

In the shadow of these political afterwords, Spicer's divided books of poetry and paratexts reaffirm his need to articulate provisional borders between insiders and outsiders—author and translator, minimalist poet and flirtatious exegete, *kreis* member and orphic speaker for a wider canon—that he can transgress in order to expose the limitations of either side's communal histories. Although recent American avant-garde poets do not necessarily retain his sense of the Logos, many have adapted his tropes of ghostly palimpsests, misdirections, and mistranslations in their own paratexts, trying to create a broader cultural context for poems without sacrificing what Spicer described as the poetry's "uncomfortable music" (*CB* 213), the gaps and disjunctions meant to astonish readers into redefining their narratives of literary frontiers.

# 4

## The Palimpsest as Communal Lyric:
## Susan Howe's Paratextual Sources

Palimpsest: A parchment or other writing-material written upon
twice, the original writing having been erased or rubbed out to
make place for the second; a manuscript in which a later writing
is written over an effaced earlier writing.
                                        —*Oxford English Dictionary*

your stylus is dipped in corrosive sublimate,
how can you scratch out

indelible ink of the palimpsest
of past misadventure?
                                        —H.D., *Trilogy*

I worried about the previous occupants of the house, their traces
burned off by daylight. . .
                        —Rosmarie Waldrop, *The Reproduction of Profiles*

The dialogue between the poet and a ghostly predecessor in Jack Spicer's
translations and homages continues in the writing of a second generation of post–
World War II avant-gardists in the palimpsest form. The postmodern palimp-
sest poem is a visual collage in which excerpts of a paratextual source are juxta-
posed on the same page space with the poet's responses to that source.

Though palimpsest originally designated one text written over an erased
source, many recent poetic palimpsests are indebted to H.D., who used the term
as a metaphor for the project of the woman poet writing through a patriarchal
cultural history to recover traces of elided female myths and signs.[1] Contempo-
rary palimpsest artists adapt that metaphor to fit a variety of agendas; they frac-

ture and recontextualize the language of a source work in order to foreground its contradictions, redirect its premises, or introduce oppositional perspectives that the source excludes. The palimpsest relation between a fractured visual poem and a more familiar source paratext, as I have suggested, recalls the anomaly of the early avant-garde manifesto that was better known than the poetry it introduced. Palimpsest in fact depends upon an audience's recognition of the paratext or its connection to a pivotal historical event in order for the reviser to present a communal narrative that is simultaneously traditional and revolutionary.

The fine edge between the familiar and the innovative is particularly hard to distinguish in palimpsests where there is no typographic indication of what words belong to each author; the resulting field of juxtaposed phrases or sentences blurs the distinction between pastiche and plagiarism. In Rosmarie Waldrop's *The Reproduction of Profiles,* a book that builds a prose-poetic narrative from distorted fragments of Wittgenstein's writings, the image of the house with new tenants might aptly symbolize the source paratext taken over by another author. Words themselves now become "negative facts" with "nonexistent mouths," capable of being "twisted for explanation" (14) in different contexts. The lack of "traces" (75) distinguishing source from revision implies that writing styles and subject positions are constructions to be appropriated as the reviser desires.

As my introductory quote by H.D. suggests, however, the idea of the poet as palimpsest artist also has ties to a Romantic lyricism that valorizes subjectivity. Her corrosive stylus evokes Blake with his acid engravings and his images of a heroic poetic ego cutting through cultural platitudes. This background is important because the subjectivity not only of the reviser but also of the "previous occupants"—the paratextual authors and narrators—comes up in unexpected ways when recent palimpsest writers have tried to create an alternate tradition for their own work. Should the same fracturing, plagiaristic techniques be applied to a source paratext that is not canonical or that the reviser feels has been misinterpreted, particularly a source that anticipates the reviser's own agenda or style? For some of the most provocative dialogues with previous occupants, I turn to the palimpsests of Susan Howe, an experimental poet whose work with paratextual source documents in compositions from the seventies through the nineties has gained her critical attention as a key figure in contemporary American avant-garde poetry.

## Lyric Postmodernist

Howe's love of visual arts, archival research, and literary scholarship are reflected in books that intermesh lines of poetic commentary with passages of a literary or historical source, her composite pages arranged in creative typographic patterns. Her poetic politics has generated intense debate because it exemplifies the conflicting postmodernist and Romantic elements of the palimpsest form. I restate those elements briefly here since the interplay between them is crucial to understanding the two forms that Howe's palimpsests take: the fragmentary grids of source words with interpolated phrases in her poetry and the poetic essays that annotate a source at length.

Howe's poetics on the one hand seems quintessentially postmodern as she adopts a language of chaotic systems, mathematical singularities, and noise.[2] In a 1990 interview, she defines her research interests as the ellipses and contradictions inherent in every source text: "It's the stutter in American literature that interests me. I hear the stutter as a sounding of uncertainty" (*B* 181). Her poetic pages combine isolated paratextual references with her own shifting pronouns, word recombinations ("uplispth," "adamap," "floted" [*S* 59]), superimposed typescripts, and multi-angled lines to create a dense collage that the reader can enter at varying points to interpret different word juxtapositions.

Unlike the Language poets with whom she was initially associated, however, she also valorizes the lyric genre as "a most compressed and lovely thing. . . . the highest form" (*B* 171), depicts the poet as an inspired "seer" (*MED* 35), and uses a vocabulary of voice and presence even though, as her commentators note, she sees subjectivity as always inscribed in specific historical contexts and language practices.[3] Despite the pronoun shifts, she returns frequently to the first person in her poetry and prose. And although history and fiction blur in these texts— her "subjects" are often literary characters that symbolize marginal identities and hidden rebellions within a nation—she nevertheless metaphorizes her palimpsests as a retrieval of lost speakers. "I wish I could tenderly lift from the dark side of history," she comments in the preface to her 1990 poetry collection, *The Europe of Trusts,* "voices that are anonymous, slighted—inarticulate" (14). "If history is a record of survivors," she asserts in *The Birth-mark,* a 1993 text of American literary history, then "Poetry shelters other voices" (47).

To recover these "other voices" in her eighties and nineties palimpsests, Howe drew first on Anglo-Irish sources but has focused increasingly on American texts from the colonial period through the late nineteenth century to expose the "Sexual, racial, and geographical separation" that accompanied various attempts to define a cultural consensus (*MED* 21). Sex or rather gender tends to subsume other categories of difference; Howe uses a discourse of feminization both for political dissidents who were silenced and for experimental writers whose texts were edited into conformity with prevailing standards: "The issue of editorial control is directly connected to the attempted erasure of antinomianism in our culture. Lawlessness seen as negligence is at first feminized and then restricted or banished" (*B* 1).[4] Culture or community often seems synonymous with a destructive patriarchy in her texts, an "iconic Collective" (*S* 65) for the "invention of law" and "the codification of money" (67). Howe's antinomianism, in turn, is more than the specific challenge to seventeenth-century Puritan ecclesiastical and civil authority from followers who believed that they were divinely enabled to distinguish the justified from the sanctified. She uses the term to denote a range of innovative language practices and personal claims of inspired authority against entrenched social orders. The desire to fracture definitions of consensus and to retrieve instances of dissent inspires her poetic palimpsests; the challenge of finding alternative definitions of poetic and political community for her marginalized dissenters produces the essays.

## Poetic Palimpsests

Howe's parameters for a source paratext in her poetic palimpsests are by now familiar: a canonical work or a historical archive that presents subjects alienated from their community in conflicts over private and public identity that Howe reads in terms of gender. Sometimes the source does so sympathetically, as in Melville's *Billy Budd, Sailor,* whose title character with his stutters and silences Howe describes as "mysteriously woman" (*B* 37). More often she argues that the paratext treats the feminine as monstrous, misinterprets its dissent, or simply ignores it, as in the wry comment she makes in an interview about her poetic reworking of Madison's *Federalist* 10 essay: "Women were just too far out of the picture to be considered a faction when our Constitution was written" (BI 22).

The dialogue with a sympathetic source that already thematizes silenced or aberrant voices offers particular insight into the remarkable creativity as well as the limitations of the poetic palimpsest genre. Howe's "Scattering As Behavior Toward Risk," published in the 1990 *Singularities* volume, adapts the *Billy Budd* story of the "Handsome Sailor" condemned to death by his commander for an inadvertent act of violence against a false accuser. Although Captain Vere knows that Budd was innocent of criminal intent, he nevertheless argues that, under the wartime Mutiny Act, the foretopman must be hanged as a disciplinary example for the crew. The sailor's death is deemed miraculous in Melville's text because of the silent motionlessness of his hanged body. Into this silence, Howe's poem openly inserts a child's protest against "Fathers" who "dare not name me" (*S* 67), a reference both to Budd's status as a foundling and to his treatment by the authoritative Vere, as her text probes the "muttering," "lamentation" (66), and "Secret fact" (70) behind the sailor's history.

The penultimate page of the *Billy Budd* palimpsest demonstrates the complexity of the text-paratext relation. The source for the page is taken from Captain Vere's speech at Budd's trial for mutiny and murder. Before looking at the manuscript variations, two passages from the Reading Text in the Hayford and Sealts edition of the story are pertinent here, the first asserting the irrelevance of compassion to the trial decision, and the second appealing to war-time exigencies:

> "Ashore in a criminal case, will an upright judge allow himself off the bench to be waylaid by some tender kinswoman of the accused seeking to touch him with her tearful plea? Well, the heart here, sometimes the feminine in man, is as that piteous woman, and hard though it be, she must here be ruled out." (111)

> "[B]efore a court less arbitrary and more merciful than a martial one, that plea [Budd's lack of criminal intent] would largely extenuate. At the Last Assizes it shall acquit. But how here? We proceed under the law of the Mutiny Act. In feature no child can resemble his father more than that Act resembles in spirit the thing from which it derives—War. In His Majesty's service—in this ship, indeed—there are Englishmen forced to fight for the King against their will. Against their conscience, for aught we know. Though as their fellow creatures some of us may appreciate their position, yet as navy officers what reck we of it? Still less recks the enemy. Our impressed men he would fain cut down in the same swath with our volunteers. As regards the enemy's naval conscripts, some of whom may even share our own abhorrence of the regicidal French Directory, it is the same on our side. War looks but to the frontage, the appearance. And the Mutiny Act, War's child, takes after the father. Budd's intent or non-intent is nothing to the purpose." (111–12)

As Howe transforms the paratext, just enough of Melville's themes and words, especially from the second passage, remain to direct the reader to the narrative while still presenting considerable interpretive difficulties (see fig. 4.1). Howe's palimpsest thus serves the twofold function of providing a well-recognized source as the guidepost for her scattered collage and defamiliarizing the paratext as her language games counterpoint the semantic slippages in Melville's own language. His narrator undercuts Vere's discourse about appearances by playing with words that look or sound alike (e.g., "martyr to martial discipline" [BB 121]) to create ironies that cannot be condensed into a single legalistic message. But where the Reading Text of Billy Budd plays on verbal excesses, Howe rewrites Vere's speech as a series of textual elisions and discontinuities. Her initial footnote to "Scattering" states that her source is not the version most readers remember but a composite Genetic Text transcribed by Hayford and Sealts from Melville's manuscript revisions of the story, with different emendations for a single passage juxtaposed with italicized editorial notes. The lines of the speech in this Genetic Text are so often interrupted that they resemble an avant-garde experiment in typography: "a ma→<a ma→from the→<from the→a martial one" (*BB* 396). This composite source, as Peter Quartermain points out (190), already exposes the closure of an authoritative text as a fiction, presenting an unfinished composition in which new formulations continually *"alter"* or even *"cancel"* the *"whole"* of a previous passage (*BB* [editorial notation] 412). We watch Melville's impressed men lose their appearance of loyalty as service to "their" king becomes service to "the" king (*BB* 396), and the seeming passivity of "serve" is itself exposed in the revision "fight for" (396).

Howe's own revisions extend the scattering process suggested in the Genetic Text, her page's visual center becoming a disorienting space in which meanings are indeed too "fluent" (*S* 69) or fluid as the distinctions among words break

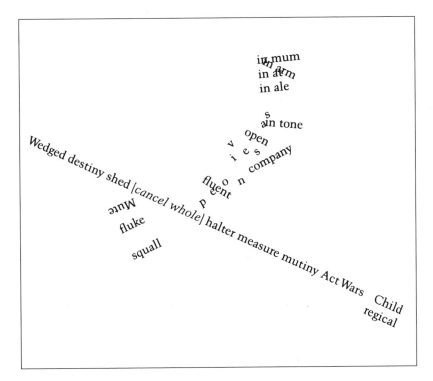

Fig. 4.1. Excerpt from Susan Howe, "Scattering As Behavior Toward Risk," *Singularities,* p. 69. Copyright 1990 by Susan Howe and Wesleyan University Press. Courtesy of University Press of New England.

down.[5] Does "s / ain tone" play on the question of Vere's sanity? The imputation of "s / in," a discourse borrowed from earlier passages on Billy's accuser, doubles with the possible appearance of Budd as a "s / ain t." But the theological context is unstable; to what referent does "in at" point? Only the drunken confusion of being "in ale"? An "ale"-ing/ailing navy lies on the brink of "mutiny." Between the "fluent" and the "Mute" is the sudden "fluke" of a "squall" or cry. As Billy Budd is hanged in Melville's text, an "inarticulate" murmur (*BB* 126) ripples through the crew. If that protest had been fully voiced, could it have helped to "shed" a "Wedged destiny" and *"cancel"* the "halter measure" (*S* 69), the discipline that required Billy's hanging?

The question of whose historical "destiny" (*S* 69) the palimpsest describes is also subtly redirected. Dropping the explicit details of the paratext's setting allows Howe to translate these mutinous undertones more fluently between national contexts, foregrounding the ambiguities already present in Melville's British naval story, a narrative that repeatedly refers back to American contexts. He offers the United States less as a revolutionary champion of the *"Rights-of-Man"* (*BB* 48) than as a continuation of strategic national silences about dissent: "Like some other events in every age befalling states everywhere, including America, the Great Mutiny was of such character that national pride along with views of policy would fain shade it off into the historical background" (*BB* 55). Howe's jumbled letter play in figure 4.1 transforms the impressed sailors into New World "peon[s]" and asks us to consider subjects relegated to background positions in our "Own political literature" (*S* 65) of "Democracy and property" (67), with "Own" also hinting at disputes over who owns the rights to articulate a national narrative, disputes that resonate ironically with the plagiaristic approach to sources in a palimpsest.

Howe's poetic scattering of the paratext seems to offer a composition by field even more radically indeterminate than the lines of Olson, her fellow New England visual poet and Melville aficionado. Yet Howe's palimpsest at the same time relies on a highly focused counterprotest to Vere's authority as she uses the arrangement of the words to reintroduce traces of the feminized petitioner in Melville's story. The penal silence, "mum" (*S* 69), that surrounds Budd's case also suggests the kinswoman ruled out of Vere's judgment and the stammered "ma"s in the Genetic Text. The "arm" in the top portion of Howe's page doubles as an armament and as an arm emanating from the word "mum," as if spatially reassembling the body of the mother beneath the military language. By separating "Child" from its context in Vere's speech and prefacing this passage with a reference to "My heavy heavy child" on the preceding page (68), Howe substitutes a living infant, a reminder of "Baby" Budd, for the metaphorical offspring of the violent father in Vere's speech ("the Mutiny Act, War's child" [*BB* 112]). It is not the foreigners of the Reading Text but the child, read through the broken words of the Genetic Text, that can be described as "regical" (*S* 69)—regic[id]al or perhaps magical in its repudiation of military discourse.

Along with the images of recovered bodies, what happens to the characters' words? The selections and omissions from the Melville paratext are curious. Howe's poem may fracture Vere's speech, but it does not use Budd's own language in the story directly; the complaint that "Fathers dare not name me" is Howe's interpolation (*S* 67). Nor are there clear excerpts from the anonymous ballad that the sailors circulate about Billy's death. With its colloquialisms and its crude printing, the ballad seems to occupy a liminal communal space between the official records of the episode and Budd's final silence. Yet the two possible references to the ballad in Howe's text, the decontextualized words "sleep" (67) and "hatchet-" (68) on different pages of the palimpsest, suggest a loss of consciousness and an excision rather than a well-articulated voice.

Even within the fictional context of the Melville story, these omissions suggest Howe's ambivalence about defamiliarizing the language of a feminized character or an alternative history through the violent scattering of the palimpsest method. In order to reconcile the palimpsest's disruptive style with the project of recovering elided subjects, she strikes a compromise, framing dense word clusters with unexpectedly clear phrases that allow readers to reorient themselves, if only temporarily, with a "story" of the "Trial and suffering / of Mercy" (*S* 64). But the omissions and interpretive frames raise questions about the politics of the poetic palimpsest strategy. Howe suggests that a palimpsest, by revealing "one poem in another we haven't seen or thought," can provide a genuinely "communal vision of poetry," an open, anti-territorial space for exchange (BI 20). The transition from portraying an official consensus riddled with dissent to placing those protests within an alternate communal history, however, continues to challenge the narrators in the poetic palimpsests.

## Essay Palimpsests

In order to define a "communal vision of poetry" when "you are curved, odd, indefinite, irregular, feminine" (*MED* 117–18), Howe alters her palimpsest format to produce the essays in *My Emily Dickinson* (1985) and *The Birth-mark* (1993). I describe these essays as an extension of her palimpsests because they are also organized as highly creative responses to specific sources. The first book, which advertises its dialogue structure in the title, writes through a poem by a predecessor whom Howe argues has been misedited and misinterpreted. The second offers Howe's imaginative speculations on paratextual passages from a series of iconoclastic American speakers or writers who questioned the premises of their contemporary communal histories.

Stylistically, the essays resemble prose poems with rhythmic patterns, alliterative sound play, and metonymic digressions. But they emphasize a project of retrieval and explication over the poetic palimpsest's fragmenting approach to its source. Howe not only distinctly transcribes quotes but also places each source at the center of an increasingly broad circle of intertexts: the literary and historical works that influenced it, the criticism that misread it, and her own lyrical tributes to its experiments.[6] She identifies so closely with these early authors that her commentary, as the essay form suggests, serves a paratextual function itself as she constructs a revolutionary tradition that guides the reader through her own poetic politics. To integrate the two halves of the essay guides, I scrutinize the choice and presentation of sources and analyze the formats of her expansive responses.

Her dialogues with Anne Hutchinson, Mary Rowlandson, Emily Dickinson, or Gertrude Stein go beyond a feminist revaluation of women writers. The issue Howe emphasizes is twofold: why such "pathfinders were women" and "why American" (*MED* 11). In *My Emily Dickinson,* she describes a search for expression within the constraints of a specific culture: "First I find myself a Slave, next I understand my slavery, finally I re-discover myself at liberty inside the confines of known necessity" (118). Howe argues that the female artist's need to "be rebellious and to distrust rebellion" (114), to dismantle institutions at the same time she remains suspicious of community-destroying violence, takes place against "the original American conflict between idealism and extremism" (74) or, more specifically, between affirmations of a new separatist community and a rhetoric of tearing down authoritative political structures.

## From Simulacrum to Record: Howe's Palimpsest Sources

As Howe affirms her own communities of American separatists, one of the key differences between the poetic and the essay palimpsests is her approach to the authenticity of the source. Her narrator in "A Bibliography of the King's Book or, Eikon Basilike," a 1989 poetic palimpsest, is intrigued by the fact that the bibliography's original subject, the text ostensibly written by King Charles I before his execution, is a "forgery" (*NM* 47).[7] The palimpsest continually substitutes new constructs for the absent authorial center, with the "ghost of a king" (48) becoming "Great Caesar's ghost" (66), vengeful Coriolanus, "failed" kings "of Judah" (72), and Christ sacrificed, as well as a series of dubious ghostwriters. "Can we ever really discover the original text?" Howe questions in the preface. "Was there ever an original poem? . . . Only by going back to the pre-scriptive level of thought process can 'authorial intention' finally be located, and then the material object has become immaterial" (50). Howe's palimpsest is a celebration of spectacle, from the masque-loving Charles who admirably plays the part of his own death scene to the fabrications of his last moments that follow it.

The author's absence in this source may not disturb Howe because she reads the transition from King Charles to Cromwell as the exchange of one patriarchal authority for another. Howe's approach to the "hidden feminine" in Melville ("Where Should the Commander Be" 3), I have asserted, is more conflicted. While the poetic palimpsest formula and the use of the Genetic Text in "Scattering As Behavior Toward Risk" make it difficult to identify the traces of a single originary source, Howe returns to Melville's writing and the supposed inspiration for his character Bartleby in a suggestively divided format in "Melville's Marginalia," the concluding sequence in *The Nonconformist's Memorial* (1993). The first section is a twenty-page collage of prose passages, quotes, and poetic palimpsests. The preface discusses scholarly concerns over the editing or erasure of Melville's marginal notes, but the politics of that editing is complicated for Howe because the almost-erased notes are misogynous in nature and the revisers may be the writer's wife or daughters.

In contrast, the essay book *The Birth-mark* directly foregrounds its anxiety over editing and republication. Though Howe acknowledges that publishing inevitably distorts a composition, she is disturbed by the fact that no "copy of the first edition of Mary Rowlandson's *Narrative* is known to exist" since "Future distortions, exaggerations, modifications, corrections and emendations may endow a text with meanings it never formed" (*B* 97), a somewhat surprising comment given Howe's experiments with her sources' language. There is similar concern about Anne Hutchinson, whose "verbal expression is barely audible in the scanty second- or thirdhand records of her two trials" (4). And when she considers Dickinson's writing, Howe "emphatically insist[s]," against Foucault, that it "does matter who's speaking" through the manuscripts to show "what *she, Emily Dickinson,* reveals of her most profound self" (20). The researcher's task is to recover the revelatory play of signification within the poet's fascicles, analyzing Dickinson's irregular line breaks and punctuation rather than the orderly stanzas of the Johnson edition of her poetry.

Preserving the exact words of these misinterpreted authors is crucial for Howe because it is linked to the possibility of recovering historical truths. As in Olson's prose commentary, a vocabulary of facticity and veracity dominates her essays. Even as she questions the concept of an idealist Truth and asserts that history is written by the victors, she also comments that "I am naive enough to hope the truth will out" through detailed research of historical archives (*B* 158), research that is all the more urgent because there is "real suffering on this little planet" (164).

## "You Noticed My Dwelling Alone": Audience in the Essays

Who is the audience for such research? In the essays, Howe offers a third alternative to images of community as an authoritarian patriarchy or a sampling of isolated innovators: she proposes an audience as a necessary party to witness and validate a poet's experiments.[8] Howe may find "a mystic separation between poetic vision and ordinary living" (*MED* 13), but assertions such as "the truth will out" imply the need for a participatory audience that can confirm the other voices that poetry shelters. It is no coincidence that both of her essay books discuss the captivity narrative written by Mary Rowlandson, a colonial woman captured by Narragansetts and later ransomed. What fascinates Howe is Rowlandson's struggle to translate an experience that challenged the premise of a beneficent Providence and a holy New World mission into terms that a Puritan audience could accept. If she deprecates Rowlandson's self-censoring, her invocation of God's sustaining power whenever the story seemed to question dogma, Howe also recognizes that it made possible the double-edged "'True History'" (*B* 89) of a woman who "saw what she did not see said what she did not say" (128) about communal exiles confronting a radical "absence of Authority" (94). Rowlandson's story in fact reshaped the reading habits of her society; Howe notes that her popular history inspired a genre of captivity narratives, even though that popularity resulted in an increasingly formulaic genre often transcribed by men (89).

Howe's interest in an author's audience extends equally to women writers whom she sees as less compromising about their message than Rowlandson. She praises Emily Dickinson, the predecessor with whose style she most closely identifies, as an innovator who kept a sense of audience in mind although almost all her poems were published posthumously. "In prose and in poetry," Howe asserts, "she explored the implications of breaking the law just short of breaking off communication with a reader" (*MED* 11). Howe is indeed kinder to one reader of Dickinson's texts during her lifetime than to any of her subsequent editors. Thomas Wentworth Higginson may have misunderstood the nature of the poet's revolt, she argues, but was nevertheless "generous" and "enthusiastic" enough (127) to respond to Dickinson's letters, enabling her to rehearse with him different role-playing games of humility and empowerment that reflect her various poetic personae. Howe quotes one particularly moving 1869 letter about what the correspondence meant for Dickinson:

> You noticed my dwelling alone—To an Emigrant, Country is idle except it be his own. You speak kindly of seeing me. Could it please your convenience to come so far as Amherst I should be very glad, but I do not cross my Father's ground to any House or town.
>
> Of our greatest acts we are ignorant—
> You were not aware that you saved my Life. To thank you in person has since been one of my few requests. (Dickinson, quoted in *MED* 126)

The reader's gaze intervenes here between images of patriarchal enclosure ("my Father's ground") and lyric exile, as if this notice might lay the foundation for a "Country" of the poet's own. Even the reader's own ignorance of his significance does not preclude the rescue. Howe closes *My Emily Dickinson* with a sympathetic history of Higginson's life, a format that preserves the reciprocal structure of their correspondence.

The image of an audience as a lyricist's country recurs in Howe's assessment of her own writing. "The one thing that would bother me," she told an interviewer in 1986, "would be if [my writing] were called elitist or precious" (FI 42). In numerous interviews and essays, she calls for a new American reading community where all the participants are rebelliously birthmarked by a willingness to experiment with different expressive forms. The style itself of her essays reflects the need for an audience to validate political or linguistic rebellion, as she combines circuitous sentences and an associative play of themes with expository arguments; the syntax and punctuation are fairly standardized and the boundaries between different paratextual sources are well marked.

Where Howe's poetic palimpsests, moreover, create new meaning through selective elision of the source's language, Howe's essays pile reference upon reference for a single paratextual phrase, as if to gather an overwhelming body of evidence for their exegesis. *My Emily Dickinson* treats the six-stanza poem "My Life had stood—a Loaded Gun—" in over a hundred pages of explication. As Dickinson develops the image of a life as a gun wielded by a masculine "Owner":

To foe of His—I'm deadly foe—
None stir the second time—
On whom I lay a Yellow Eye—
Or an emphatic Thumb—

(quoted in *MED* 34)

The passage becomes, in Howe's reading:

> Northern women, children, the maimed, infirm, and old men, waited at home until war was done. A Slave was often referred to as a child, a Woman as a girl. An original Disobedience: A girl in bed alone sucking her thumb. *Thumb:* short thick first or most preaxial digit of the human hand differing from the four fingers in having greater freedom of movement and being opposable to the other fingers. *Thumb* and *Gnome* have silent letters and rhyme wrongly with *Gun* and *whom.* For Freudians, thumb and gun are phallic and the same. Without a thumb it would be hard to grip a gun. The thumb helps my fingers grip, helps to turn the pages of a book. *All thumbs—*

> Awkward. *Under the thumb:* under control of. *Thumb:* To feel point press attack . . . to play. To thumb one's nose at the collective wisdom of the ages. Wives and slaves were thumbs. In the nineteenth century a mark made with the inked thumb was used for identification of an illiterate person. Thumb rhymes with dumb. *Thumb* a nursery word rhymes crookedly with 'time' riddled back to Jack Horner who sat in his corner, eating a Christmas Pie. He put in his thumb pulled out a plum and said "What a good boy am I!" Good Uncle Tom. Was Jack put in the corner because he was wrong or dumb? What had he done? Back around to *foe* and *Master* and Jack the Giant Killer climbing his beanstalk ladder to hear the *"Fie, foh, and fum,"* of Edgar/Tom's mad song, "I smell the blood of a British man. / Be he alive or be he dead, / I'll grind his bones to make my bread." Jack, and Jacob the *Bible's* poet, were both ladder-watchers. Tom Thumb ("Your Gnome") was little but as powerful as David the other biblical poet, who slew Goliath with a sling-shot. Cover the touch-hole of a cannon with your thumb. She, GUN-THUMB-YEL-LOW EYE-BULLET-POET-GNOME is emphatic. Dauntless predator and protector. (*MED* 119)

This brilliant sequence manipulates the audience masterfully. Although the dense sound play makes the passage itself resemble artillery fire, it does not target the reader with a focused polemic but rather with a series of facts and suppositions connected metonymically by "crooked" rhymes that evoke Dickinson's own slant rhyme poetry. Far from thumbing her nose at collective wisdom, Howe uses widely accessible references here: the Bible, Shakespeare, nursery rhymes, and fairy tales. Much of the passage uses simple, often monosyllabic words, while nevertheless managing to convey Civil War political overtones of opposition, freedom, and Uncle Toms in the images of disobedient girls. She captures both the violence of domestic gender constraints and the implications of Dickinson's use of a masculine rhetoric of "GUNS AND GRACE" (46) alongside tropes of self-deprecating diminution. To play is to attack; a disruptive lyric persona shifting between positions of marginalization and authority, Howe argues, can be used as a political weapon.

Yet Howe's own style, as I suggest, also predisposes the reader to accept its premises. In contrast to the scattered phrases that readers must connect in the poetic palimpsests, the pace of this essay passage discourages intervention or protest; with few transitions, the reader plunges from one rapid-fire sequence to the next. The conflicting poses in "Dauntless predator and protector" or Howe's juxtaposition of slaves and wives—an associative leap that warrants qualification—slip past more or less unquestioned in context of the familiar allusions and the translation of an original crime into the childhood memory of sucking one's thumb. The impression the reader retains is not even of a specific thesis so much as an infectious delight in Howe's transformations of Dickinson's tightly controlled lines into these exegetical effusions.

The essays' elaborate interpretive frames may be a safeguard against the vulnerability of the moment of publication when "What I put into words is no longer my possession" (*MED* 13) and can be distorted by the most well-intentioned reader. *My Emily Dickinson* and *The Birth-mark* each offers different analyses of the public role of antinomian experiments. The earlier book treats an isolated lyricist as the guardian of communal goals; the second expands these discussions to include openly public declarations of dissent. If neither book offers a prescriptive formula for the new lyric, that is because Howe refuses to "relegate women to what we 'should' or 'must' be doing" (*MED* 13) by reducing questions of audience address to simplistic oppositions. The two books, as they echo and respond to each other, are best read as stages in Howe's representations of the poet's relation to her audience.

## Lyric Recovery

Of the two essay books, the earlier study of Dickinson seems the more unusual choice for defining a communal lyric. By the time *My Emily Dickinson* was published in 1985, the Amherst poet had already become an icon in American feminist criticism as a self-isolated experimenter, whether in Sandra M. Gilbert and Susan Gubar's description of Dickinson as a "private spider artist" stitching dramatic costumes for herself (639), an image to which Howe takes exception, or in Adrienne Rich's portrait of a poet who produced her texts literally and symbolically "on [her] own premises" (27). Howe herself admires Dickinson's reluctance to publish poems and her ability to create a lyric space in which "communal identity" can be temporarily "lost" (*MED* 70).

That detachment, paradoxically, is the key to Howe's reading of an artist whose insights speak "'for all of us'" (*MED* 137). Howe argues that Dickinson's isolation and her experiments with multiple self-constructions make her a fitting exemplar of a New England tradition of separatist controversies and introspective scrutiny. Her texts echo the "restless contradictions" (38) embedded in Puritan injunctions to strive actively for grace and to accept one's utter dependence on the deity, or to be willing to defy established civil authority and yet to form a stable model city in the wilderness.[9] Howe then places Dickinson's texts in the wider context of a national revolutionary legacy. She reads "My Life had stood—" as a "pioneer's terse epic" (35) combining a personal narrative ("Dickinson herself, waiting in corners of neglect for Higginson to recognize her ability and help her to join the ranks of other published American poets" [76]) with a history of revolutionary visions of community that were implemented through violence:

> *My Life:* The American continent and its westward moving frontier. Two centuries of pioneer literature and myth had insistently compared the land to a virgin woman (bride and queen). Exploration and settlement were pictured in terms of masculine erotic discovery and domination of alluring/threatening feminine territory.
>
> . . . . . . . . . . . . . . . . . . . . . . . . . . . . . . . . . . . . . . . . . . . . . . . . . . . . . . . .
>
> *My Life:* The United States in the grip of violence that threatened to break apart its original Union.
>
> *My Life:* A white woman taken captive by Indians.
>
> *My Life:* A slave.
>
> (76)

*"My Life":* the phrase evokes all the paradoxes in Howe's overwritten palimpsest subjects to be recovered. The national lyricist Howe/Dickinson speaks for My Life always implicated in Ours, or Hers, or Theirs without the reassurance of any consensus. There is no "original Union" behind the Civil War in this expansive discussion built on Dickinson's two words, only a site of different power struggles and myths. The frontiersman confronts a "virgin" territory that is also already inhabited by the "Indians" who will figure in the captivity narratives, while the captivity plots of suffering and redemption are bracketed ironically by slave histories.

Yet by collapsing autobiography and political history, Howe makes the relation between author and audience more reciprocal. The poet may need an audience to respond to textual experiments, but the poet also becomes the witness of the community's experience: "Dickinson was expert in standing in corners, expert in secret listening and silent understanding" (*MED* 116). As the "My Life" palimpsest expansions suggest, moreover, she is an expert among failed followers, the seer who preserves a separatist vision that is in danger either of being lost or of falling into destructive negation. The idealism of the founding fathers, Howe contends, "broke down in some way under the strain of worldly ambition that clashed with morbid fear and merciless introspection" (45) or else degenerated into the politics of a John Brown: "Liberators and the righteous were, as always, burning, looting and destroying" (74). In contrast, Howe's Dickinson as Gun challenges myths about both rebels and patriarchs, but her battles are also described in section headings of "ARCHAEOLOGY" (37) and "ARCHITECTURE OF MEANING" (75) that emphasize the poet as the reviser/rediscoverer of shared landmarks.

_My Emily Dickinson_ concludes with a dramatic version of the poet-legislator reconciling revolutionary negation and affirmation:

> Poetry is the great stimulation of life. Poetry leads past posses-
> sion of self to transfiguration beyond gender. Poetry is redemption
> from pessimism. Poetry is affirmation in negation, ammunition in
> the yellow eye of a gun that an allegorical pilgrim will shoot straight
> into the quiet of Night's frame. Childe Roland at the moment of
> sinking down with the sun, like Phaeton in a ball of flame, sees his
> visionary precursor peers ringed round him waiting. (138)

The original Phaeton in his arrogance nearly consumed the earth and was struck down for his transgression. Browning's Childe Roland is haunted by the wraiths of predecessors who have failed their quest. But in Howe's revision, Dickinson is greeted by the approving community of peers that she did not have in her lifetime, "visionary precursor[s]" who accept her lyrical rebellion within their own tradition. Poetry's revolutionary value, Howe suggests, lies in its use as a tool both for exploring multiple "POSSIBILITIES" (76) of _My/Our Life_ and for targeting blind spots in the new communal allegories, the two halves, in other words, of the palimpsest project of recovery and scattering or recontextualization.

The authorial tone in passages like the Childe Roland segment clearly insists on Howe's own status as inspired bard. How persuasively does Howe/Dickinson move from _my_ to _our_ communal exemplar? The composite poetic protagonist in _My Emily Dickinson_ is compelling not simply because she chooses her own premises but because she comes as close as any Howe palimpsest character to choosing absolute ones—Art, Originality—words that Howe uses sparingly with other authors. She nevertheless refuses to isolate Dickinson's example. Howe prefaces _My Emily Dickinson_ with a discussion of Gertrude Stein, "an influential patron of the arts" who "eagerly courted publicity, thrived on company, and lived to enjoy her own literary celebrity" (11). The two experimental authors, she asserts, are not opposites but complements: "Dickinson and Stein meet each other along paths of the Self that begin and end in contradiction" (11), the challenge of making literary history new, both "re-invent[ing]" a language and "restor[ing] the original clarity of each word-skeleton" (11). The research into Dickinson's manuscripts, Howe acknowledges, inspired her next essay collection, _The Birth-mark: Unsettling the Wilderness in American Literary History_, whose central heroine openly confronts the political and spiritual authority of her critics.

## Public Trespasses

Howe depicts Anne Hutchinson, "the rose at the threshold of _The Birth-mark_" (21), as both exemplar and exile, an un-settler whose New England brand of separatism, which Howe links to her language use, could not be incorporated within Winthrop's communal covenant. In the context of Howe's own essay palimpsests, it is symbolic that Hutchinson's disruptions began with public exegesis: she held mixed meetings of men and women in her home to explain the sermons given at church. She was put on trial after the gatherings increased and her interpretations began to deviate from Puritan orthodoxy, to the point of suggesting that many Massachusetts ministers may not have been truly saved. Although she often out-argued her less dexterous accusers, she was excommunicated and banished for the heretical claim that she derived her insights from immediate personal revelation. Howe reads this history as the quintessential dilemma of the articulate dissenter found guilty of speaking from her own inspiration.

Whereas Howe sees Dickinson protecting a lost ideal in minimalist lyrics, however, she links Hutchinson's speech more directly to contemporary changes in her community. Howe is intrigued by the argument that Hutchinson's language represents the transition between an older English used by her judges and a distinctively American speech. She cites an article by Patricia Caldwell on New England speech patterns:

> [T]rial documents suggest that Mrs. Hutchinson was neither purposely deceiving nor hallucinating, and that her words cannot fairly be ascribed to mere stubbornness, hysteria, and personal assertiveness, nor even to a poor education. They suggest that Mrs. Hutchinson was speaking what amounts to a different language—different from that of her adversaries, different even from that of John Cotton—and that other people may have been speaking and hearing as she was, and that what happened to them all had serious literary consequences in America. (Quoted in *B* ix–x)

In the assertion that "other people may have been speaking and hearing as she was," the stereotype of a distraught woman producing monstrous or isolated expressions gives way to a founder who is more uniquely New England than her judges and who articulates a future America. In the book's chapters, Howe readily supplies fellow un-settlers who have influenced her own poetics, a range of voices from four centuries of American literary and historical paratexts as well as British Romantic sources.

As the epigraph page indicates, the book's title places these essays in dialogue with Howe's poetic palimpsest in "Scattering As Behavior Toward Risk." The birthmark reference is from *Billy Budd, Sailor* by way of Hawthorne, as Melville turned the symbolic mark on the face of a beautiful woman, a mark whose removal causes her death, into a signifier of linguistic difference by linking it to Budd's speech impediment of stammering. As if in answer to the omissions in

"Scattering," Howe inserts in *The Birth-mark* direct quotes from Melville's Budd and from the "mutinous" ballad "without a known author" produced by his shipmates (*B* 37). For all the play with language, she frames the words of her marginalized or dissenting historical sources just as carefully. Howe emphasizes her "postmodern editorial decision" (39), for example, to transform the last paragraph of a letter by the arrested Quaker Mary Dyer into a poem, but in fact she maintains the clarity of the passage's opening and concluding phrases to bracket her rearrangements of intervening words, and even the fragments preserve a clear sense of a single voice, with "I" or "me" recurring in almost every line (122).

As if emulating Hutchinson's mixed gatherings, Howe includes more extended paratextual sources from canonical male authors than in *My Emily Dickinson,* presenting these sources as alternate versions of American dissenters' documents. She quotes from the New England ecclesiastical history of "provincial nonconformist author" Cotton Mather (*B* 30) or from the letters of F. O. Matthiessen to his lover, texts of a homosexuality that the scholar "banished," in Howe's freighted phrase, from his public life (13). The digressive structure of the chapter essays contributes to the un-settling effect. Though each chapter has several central paratexts that ground its arguments, the response to an individual source is interrupted by questions, related sources, and seemingly oppositional narratives, as when Howe juxtaposes Hutchinson's trial testimony with statements from the autobiography of one of her accusers, Thomas Shepard, to expose the conflicts in his own self-representations. The discussion of a single author frequently takes place across chapter divisions as each new reference adds more complexity to the palimpsestic recovery process.

In tone and form, the book is even more of a heteroglossia. It evokes popular culture genres—detective novels, ghost stories, and confessions—and the last section is an interview presenting the poet-critic to her audience. The book's language alternates between metaphoric, alliterative sentences ("Rungs between escape and enclosure are confusing and compelling" [*B* 46]) and faintly parodic scholarly jargon ("the positivism of literary canons and master narratives . . . the legitimation of power" [46]) as Howe, for many years an academic outsider, asserts her own standing within a community of literary critics. The claims of poetic authority, however, remain the most peremptory: "[Dickinson] is one of the greatest poets who ever wrote in English" (19). Howe as palimpsest artist interjects herself into the text more frequently, linking the subjective *I* to declarations of local and national community through the source documents that provide, if not origins, at least the "originary" debates over communal covenants: "Now I know that the arena in which Scripture battles raged among New Englanders with originary fury is part of our current American system and events, history and structure" (47).

These affirmations of the authorial *I* are partly a defensive reaction. If *The Birth-mark* is one of Howe's most sustained attempts to reconcile lyric experimentation with a communal audience, it also explores the consequences of losing control over one's words. The fable of a rebel who speaks out in public is a cautionary one. Hutchinson is indeed punished, Howe asserts, because she embodies New England history too closely; her public self-defense makes her a "community scapegoat" who is "humbled" by her judges for their own "Transgression" of separatism in coming to the New World (*B* 52).[10] Instead of Dickinson's legacy of nearly eighteen hundred poems, moreover, Hutchinson leaves far fewer traces of her public speech. Howe speculates that records of Hutchinson's trial may have been destroyed in a 1765 riot against her great-great-grandson, who was then the chief justice and royal lieutenant governor as well as the author of a history of the Massachusetts colony. As she imagines the event, the colonists' rebellion against political authority and its archival histories literally consumes the traces of Hutchinson's earlier antinomian dissent that had helped to articulate the difference between New and Old England. In this symbolic erasure by the new separatists, Howe finds an ironic echo of the sacrificial absence imposed on Hutchinson by her original accusers.

The most disturbing question that Howe raises is whether Hutchinson did have a choice between public and private discourse. She had tried to maintain the distinction at her trial: "'It is one thing for me to come before a public magistracy and there to speak what they would have me to speak and another when a man comes to me in a way of friendship privately there is difference in that'" (*B* 13). Without comment, Howe quotes Winthrop's response: "'What if the matter be all one'" (13). If private speech is always a public, political act, how does one formulate a language on one's own premises? Howe's ambivalence toward this exposure is captured in a particularly telling interview remark:

> I've recently been editing the question-from-the-audience section of a book *[The Politics of Poetic Form: Poetry and Public Form]* that consists of lectures some of us gave for a course Charles Bernstein gave at the New School last year. Someone in the audience said, "Is anything real? I personally don't know if anything is real." In the text, in a printed bracket, there is the word *laughter.* During the real event, the audience must have laughed, and I was too preoccupied at the time to notice. When I saw *laughter* in brackets, it made me angry. (*B* 164)

Although the laughter might have indicated a number of reactions, Howe interprets it as a challenge to the existence of history outside of our narratives and to poetry's involvement with that history. This is the context for her irate rebuttal, "There is real suffering on this little planet. . . . There are things that must never be forgotten. It's not a laughing matter" (164). The modifier "real" in "real event" foregrounds the poetic lecture performance or the focused question and answer format rather than the flippant audience response that enters now as a bracketed intrusion. Yet the audience's failure to grasp the implications of the presentation becomes a sign of past and present communal degeneration: "Why are we such a violent nation? Why do we have such contempt for powerlessness? . . . I am trying to understand what went wrong when the first Europeans stepped on shore here" (164). It is the same bitterness that H.D. expressed about the difficulty of writing through the "indelible ink of . . . past misadventure" (512), put in stark terms of truth versus illusion, rebellion versus complicity—with the audience suggestively ranged on the side of complicity.

To ensure that the reader grasps the significance of its historical analogies, *The Birth-mark* repeatedly rephrases its framing commentary on the source paratexts. In the book's chapter on Mary Rowlandson, for instance, Howe intermeshes quotes from the captivity narrative with a terse summary of historical events and a present-tense series of interpretations, each of her commentaries playing with readers' expectations of genre conventions. If statements like "[Rowlandson] and her children with some nieces, nephews, and neighbors crossed into absence on February 10, 1675" (124) suggest the inadequacy of a statistical history to describe the captivity experience, Howe readily translates the disappearance for us: "This is a crime story. Remember, captives and captors are walking together beyond the protective reduplication of Western culture through another epoch far off" (124). To forestall predictable interpretations of villains and victims, Howe underscores the narrative as the site of multiple crimes of erasure and constraint as if our remembering those different layers were the first step in remembering another kind of communal historiography.

To make the process of remembering more tangible, Howe scrutinizes whenever possible the material traces of her sources.[11] While many of the poetic palimpsests refer to manuscripts and marginalia, *The Birth-mark* includes some of Howe's most extensive analysis of the physical details of various manuscript pages. Where *My Emily Dickinson* discusses reprinted facsimiles of the poet's script, *The Birth-mark*'s chapter on Dickinson describes the folds and embossed seals of the stationery she used as part of a "fictitious real" that she incorporated into a poem's imagery and visual layout (142). Or rather, the materiality of this unpublished manuscript realizes the poet's fictions of audience, becoming the true correspondence between Dickinson and the reader who wishes to retrieve every implication of her language experiments: "These manuscript books and sets represent the poet's 'letter to the world'" (152), a metaphor, as Howe notes (153), that recalls Spicer's argument that Dickinson's prose letters are a variation of her poetic forms.

To extend the act of recovery and augmentation beyond a dialogue between poets, Howe uses images of marginal annotation to recast the palimpsest artist as a symbol for the reader. Her own experience, in Coleridge's phrase, as a "'library-cormorant'" fishing for eclectic paratexts (*B* 26) inspires *The Birth-mark*'s chapter *"Submarginalia"* that echoes Olson's outlines for a cultural bibliography actively reassembled by the reader. Howe's library, however, is not simply open to investigation. The volumes come already annotated by previous readers, each revision bracketed by the next: "Every source has another center so is every creator" (39). Coleridge scribbles notes in the margins on borrowed books, his daughter rereads his library to edit his writing, and Howe reinterprets the significance of her editorial project. Puritan history becomes a vision of Cotton Mather searching his own favorite library volumes for excerpts for the 800-page *Magnalia Christi Americana* that Howe reads as a series of New England "Marginalia" (30), a mix of historical accounts, scriptural commentary, quotes, poems, and anagrammatic play that would influence subsequent literary fishers such as Hawthorne and Melville. Howe's emphasis on readerly annotation as writing allows multiple definitions of text-paratext dialogues at the margins of American literary history, as opposed to the inarticulate audience laughter that Howe saw as questioning the premise of a public forum on poetic politics.

With its emphasis on lines of influence and descent, the chapter on submarginalia, despite its intertwined narrative segments, is very much an articulation of literary forms in time, mapping consecutive responses and counter-responses to a source. Howe's attraction to the palimpsest structure in both her poems and essays may be rooted in the same underlying sense of linearity. Palimpsest seems to create a simultaneous visual intertext of source and revision on the same page space, and yet the reader must first recover the language play and history of the source text to understand the significance of the collage. This is why Howe provides contextual references in the readerly prefaces to several of her poetic palimpsests if the source's history is less widely known; the essays go much further, offering ample bibliographies, acknowledgments, and text abbreviation keys in addition to historical background. Whether one believes that Howe's statement "Sometimes I know you just from reading" (*B* 39) signifies the recovery of marginal perspectives or a creative fiction, she nevertheless makes sure that her audience can retrace her steps in order to appreciate the strategy of the palimpsest form.

In the metaphor of marginalia, do Howe's images of treasured library volumes contradict her sense of rebelling against tradition? Her paratextual choices in both the poetic and essay palimpsests attest that the most innovative reversals and recoveries take place not against a monologic source, whether a canonical history or an over-edited composition, but against one whose nuances and ambiguities match the complexity of the poetic revisions. It is Howe's way of reinforcing her point that a heavily inscribed textual landscape full of errors and visionary examples, rather than a mythically blank wilderness, allows the poet to display the unsettling originality of her own work—and to provide material for the next reviser. In a 1987 review, George F. Butterick, Olson's editor, pays her the fitting tribute of proposing her own work as a paratextual source document in the process of transformation: "I imagined her manuscripts, worksheets, all but illegible with revision" ("Mysterious" 312). The act of scattering/recovering a poem from Howe's genetic texts and marginalia would be a worthy challenge for the future palimpsest artist.

# 5

## "The Constitution of Public Space": Charles Bernstein's Language Paratexts

While Howe's palimpsests reconstruct communal traditions through early source texts, Charles Bernstein's paratexts focus more directly on definitions of a public role for contemporary avant-garde poetry. He emphasizes poetry as a compositional process that "explores the constitution of public space as much as representing already formed constituencies; risks its audience as often as assumes it; refuses to speak for anyone as much as fronting for a self, group, people, or species" (*MW* 304). To trace his own involvement with specific poetics forums, Bernstein is well known as the cofounder of the New York poetics journal *L=A=N=G=U=A=G=E,* first published in 1978; its title gave critics an umbrella term for a group of experimental authors who wrote prolifically on the politics of poetic form. Bernstein himself has produced over twenty books of poetry complemented by extensive essays and lectures. These paratexts are anthologized in *Content's Dream* (1986), *A Poetics* (1992), and a recent selection of new essays and interviews mixed with poems, entitled simply *My Way* (1999). Bernstein's essays must be read in close dialogue with his poetry, not only because of their creative formats—his trademark blend of academic arguments, improvisations, and humorous asides—but also because the essay paratexts articulate most clearly the conflict between risking and representing a communal identity that he ascribes to a "public" poetry.

### L=A=N=G=U=A=G=E and Its Paratexts

Since Bernstein as a poet and an editor has been closely involved with a circle of writers that publicized themselves through their essays, some background of that paratextual history is necessary. L=A=N=G=U=A=G=E or Language writing developed from a series of innovative poetry and poetics little magazines on both the East and West Coasts in the seventies and eighties.[1] The poetics essays published in these journals and later anthologized in *The L=A=N=G=U=A=G=E Book, Writing/Talks, In the American Tree, Total Syntax, Code of Signals,* or *Content's*

*Dream* adapt diverse sources—literary Marxism, Wittgensteinian philosophy, structuralism, and poststructuralism—and have gained as much scholarly attention as the poetry, if not more. While acknowledging the essays' varied theoretical approaches, critics associate poets like Bernstein, Andrews, Ron Silliman, Barrett Watten, Lyn Hejinian, Rosmarie Waldrop, or Rae Armantrout, to name only a few, with a loosely shared project in their interrogations of syntactic and semantic conventions. Many of the essays, particularly those from a more Marxist perspective, argue that the disruption of standardized grammar, referentiality, and lyric subjectivity is an inherently ideological project, since language constitutes rather than reflects social patterns of meaning.

The authors place their poetic forms in dialogue with those of early-twentieth-century avant-gardists like Stein, Pound, and Williams, as well as postwar authors such as Olson and Ashbery, at the same time that they interrogate the reification of the label "Avant-garde" as a "Commodity" (Sherry 166).[2] To heighten the connection with earlier avant-gardes, I would argue that few contemporary movements have produced both such disruptive poetry and such detailed, even proscriptive, paratexts on the social implications of writing and reading practices,[3] while often presenting those arguments through loose associations, paragrams, and typographic play. Bernstein describes such essays as the *"continuation of poetry by other means"* (AP 160).

Yet scholarship on Language paratexts, even while noting their unconventional formats, still tends to treat them more as glosses for the poetry than as one half of a creative conversation that undercuts the distinction between literature and criticism. Among the exceptions, Marjorie Perloff's "Essaying: Hot and Cool" examines the mixture of discourses and the punning multiplication of meanings in Bernstein's *Content's Dream* essays as an extension of his poetic style. Both Michel Delville and Stephen Fredman, in the conclusions of their books on American prose poetry, discuss the mix of literature and theory in Language essays. In *The Marginalization of Poetry*, Language poet Bob Perelman underscores the formal and thematic range of the paratexts as well as the ways in which the poetry often qualifies the essays. He stops short of characterizing paratexts, particularly the more programmatic and syntactically normative ones, as a necessary complement to the poetry because the goal of Language writing is to break down the distinction between author and reader, a boundary that a poetics statement or manifesto implicitly reinforces (36).

Precisely because the distinction between author and reader has persisted in Language writing, I would like to reexamine the shifts in audience address in the early paratexts to emphasize their importance to the poetry. The pages of Andrews and Bernstein's *L=A=N=G=U=A=G=E*, for example, may at first give the impression of a correspondence among a Spicerian *kreis* whose members recognize each other's arguments. The truism that the journal's prose-poetic essays closely resembled the poems they reviewed was acknowledged in the journal itself; one participant, the poet John Taggart, complains in a letter in the second issue that the reviews fail to make an already difficult poetry accessible to readers unfamiliar with the style. Though other writers challenged Taggart's assumptions, the complaint reveals a sense of the double function of these essays: to circulate poetic strategies among a small group of interested peers but also to publicize new styles and agendas for curious readers from slightly different literary backgrounds.

These early $L=A=N=G=U=A=G=E$ paratexts gesture toward a wider reading public, albeit with ambivalence. The name $L=A=N=G=U=A=G=E$ itself is both consciously avant-garde and generic; without the Dada typography, an intensive focus on language would define any literary movement. The authors dismantle literary conventions in essays with mock-formulaic titles of "Notes" and "Statements"; they mix references to vanguard authors with better-known literary and philosophical works. They emphasize their marginal status outside mainstream publishing venues and political agendas while making ambitious statements about the social implications of their language critique. "The social function of the language arts, especially the poem," Ron Silliman contends, "place them in an important position to carry the class struggle *for* consciousness to the level *of* consciousness" (131). Barrett Watten, reviewing Robert Grenier's boxed poem cards in *Sentences,* asserts more playfully that this rearrangeable text "might be the only constitution possible for the republic in which one would want to live" although "'it changes nothing' to note this" (237). Some $L=A=N=G=U=A=G=E$ authors prompt an audience's interest by explaining their poetic devices, asking directly for reader response, or couching the possibility of open participatory choices in strings of imperative sentences. "Systematically derange the language," Bernadette Mayer exhorts the would-be experimenter in a sampling of workshop assignments. "Rewrite someone else's writing. Maybe someone formidable" (80).

Bernstein's own paratexts from his earliest essays to his later articles embody these conflicts—between instructing an audience and assuming its participation and between a rhetoric of public reform and one of marginalization—that characterize many of the contributions to $L=A=N=G=U=A=G=E.$ Bernstein can argue for a writing that "calls the reader to action, questioning, self-examination: to a reconsideration and remaking of the habits, automatisms, conventions, beliefs through which, and only through which, we see and interpret the world" (*CD* 233).[4] At other times he concedes his distance from a mass audience:

> [N]ow that I am poet-professor at the University at Buffalo, I have
> retreated to an Ivory Tower, removed from the daily contact I used
> to have, as a poet-office worker in Manhattan, with the broad masses

of the American people . . . the ones that I used to meet at down-
town poetry readings and art openings. (*MW* 5–6)

These mixed claims produce unusual manifestos. In "Introjective Verse," a
response to Olson's "Projective Verse," Bernstein reverses the direction of Olson's
open parenthetical marks to emphasize the oppositional status of his own poet-
ics, a tongue-in-cheek celebration of "Rejected" authors (*MW* 110) who do not
necessarily wish to come to the mainland's shore. Bernstein promises in this
manifesto to avoid "drama and epic" (110) and to "teac[h] nothing" (111). His
essays with their versatile narrative styles and self-satire call attention to the con-
structedness of their didactic personae; they invite us, as in Spicer's notes, to
question the exegete's authority. Yet Bernstein's essays are also some of the most
straightforwardly explanatory paratexts that I discuss in this study. They present
coherent arguments in fairly linear formats, offering detailed theoretical models
for reading Language poetry and explications of its cultural significance. In what
sense, then, can these paratexts be described either as the continuation of the
poetry by other means or as a necessary complement to that poetry?

## Between Impermeability and Absorption

One of Bernstein's best known essays, "Artifice of Absorption" from *A Poetics,*
suggests a vocabulary for stylistic differences in audience address that can be used
to analyze his poetry and paratexts. Adapting Michael Fried's descriptions of
"absorption" in eighteenth-century painting, Bernstein debates the value of an
"absorptive" writing, often (but not exclusively) a transparent style that is "en-
grossing" or "spellbinding" (29), drawing the reader smoothly into its narrative,
versus an "antiabsorptive" or "impermeable" writing style that foregrounds lin-
guistic artifice, making the reader intensively conscious of his or her own pro-
cess of interpretation. The antiabsorptive mode seems the clear model for Lan-
guage poetics and yet Bernstein's essay title emphasizes that absorptive writing
is just as artful a strategy. The interdependence of the two styles is developed in
the relation between Bernstein's poetry and his essay paratexts.

His poetry vividly demonstrates the revisionary techniques of an antiabsorptive
art. He makes overly familiar signifiers in an American landscape new by using
a "contextual disruption" (*RR* 44) that distorts the meaning of a phrase by sur-
rounding it with different interpretive frames.[5] Bernstein's America is a geogra-
phy of misappropriated textual references, sites of both loss and semantic aug-
mentation. Standing in New York, he deflates Whitman's persona as well as
Olson's epic hero into "I, minimus of Amsterdam," a performer whose vanish-
ing act doesn't bode well for the fate of either the poet's private "body" or the
"body" politic (*S* 168). A quote in *Parsing* takes the reader to Gertrude Stein's

garden of American modernism in which sons drag their fathers to landmark trees, but instead of well-known markers, Bernstein's reader finds only word thickets that are "bounded by disruption" (*RR* 45). Words are units of exchange whose value is perpetually negotiated by Bernstein's narrator-traders, the clichés we expect comically inflated into surprises: "Funny $: making a killing on / junk bonds and living to peddle the tale / (victimless rime)" (*DC* 10).

There are, in fact, victims and villains in these landscapes, particularly officials mouthing the can-do patriotic truisms of the Reagan era that Bernstein denounces for concealing their social costs. But these characters are portrayed as subject positions in a series of political, economic, and medical jargons. Personal names intrude only as soap opera fragments without a frame: "Julie grows attached to an abandoned baby. . . . Rob sees red when Laura goes blond" (*II* 26). "I" and "you" are equally shifting constructs in the texts, as the reader becomes in turn the addressee of an intimate letter, a fractured commercial, a self-help pitch, or a false clue. One narrator teasingly tries to "bond the cement between us" even as he insists, "What I want to bring across to you, Buddy / is the vanity of conceits" (*RT* 71). "I'd wager you've / had it by now," another sighs solicitously about the reader caught in a poem's "speculative bonfire" (*DC* 32). "I'd give you credit / for that," he offers, "—but credit never satisfied / you" (32), if "you" are looking for a stable currency of fixed meanings in his verbal trades.

For all the humor, a defensive tone toward that "you" in Bernstein's poetry texts has only grown stronger, as his narrators suggest that the invitation to participate in these language games is rarely accepted by readers. "You look so quiet there it seems a shame to disturb you," one narrator grumbles in *Controlling Interests* (1980) after trying to project his points through a megaphone (56). To be within *"Ear Shot"* of auditors in *Rough Trades* (1991) is still to feel "marooned" (61), and "There appears to be a receiver off the hook" at the beginning of *Dark City* (1994). "Not," the narrator adds, "that / you care" (9).

The concern that the political implications of these language games may not be communicated explains why Bernstein's paratexts have become more elaborate and more integrated within the poetic texts. The same impulse motivates his most disjunctive poems and his clearest, most "absorptive" essays: a desire to educate readers about their position as consumer-subjects, not only making them aware of the ideology behind the linguistic choices made by publishing houses or broadcast networks but encouraging them to look for new forms of expression. As Bernstein defends the relatively conventional formats of his paratexts in a poetics forum from 1983:

> [I]t's very hard for us, for me, to get over the desire for this elegant, seamless, logical discourse when writing criticism, because for one

thing it has a real power. People all of a sudden start to listen to what you say when you talk in that language. I don't think by any means one should abandon that field. Because I think that to cede that power only to people who want to use it for things that you disagree with is politically foolish. (*CD* 447)

He proposes an absorptive paratextual writing that conceals the process of its own composition as one strategy among many, more a concession to the reader's conventional tastes than the poet's choice of expression. The comment, however, that "entering into the discourse of power is painful, if you have ears, because power is crude" (452) links an absorptive discourse to a loss of artistic discrimination, particularly in light of his attention to the sound of poetry. If Bernstein's early writing plays on the differences between essay and poetry, as he brings his texts and paratexts into closer dialogue, he develops subtler nuances of audience address that combine impermeable and absorptive techniques.

## Early Conversations

The formal distinction between text and paratext, as I have suggested, is more marked in the seventies and early eighties writing, although both genres are clearly creative formats. The poetry features abrupt transitions and images of absence or displacement, the visual layout sometimes as sparse as a few sentences clustered at the center of a page:

I'm separated.

I would put myself in suspended animation.

I was never home.

(RR 23)

From whom or what is the speaker separated, and what is the rest of the conditional phrase for placing oneself in suspension? This parody of a confessional lyric in *Parsing* (1976) plays on omitted or negative descriptions to elide any trace of a domestic history.

The paragraph-style passages of other early poems vary from jumbled narrative segments to syntactic collisions between phrases: "One a problem with a fragment sitting. Wave I stare as well at that only as if this all and not form letting it but is it" (*RR* 148). This excerpt from *Poetic Justice* (1979) is almost completely non-referential unless the "problem with a fragment" or "not form" becomes a description of the poem's own difficulty. The reader can break up word groups temporarily, but an arrangement such as "I stare as well at that" has no antecedent, and the grammatical function of individual words is unclear; is "Wave" a noun or an imperative? While a period normally closes a declarative statement, this "not form" ends in its own interrogation—"but is it."—the parts unable to project a cohesive whole.

In his essays and lectures from the seventies and early eighties, in contrast, Bernstein appears more concerned with the clarity that the poetry challenges, even though many of the essays were published in Language-oriented little magazines that presupposed a fairly sympathetic audience. By transplanting phrases between the poetry and paratexts, he invites readers to contrast the roles and formats of the two genres. *Content's Dream,* for example, the title of Bernstein's first essay collection, appears as an italicized phrase in his poetry book *The Sophist.* Hank Lazer glosses *content's dream* as the illusion that a composition can have a content separate from its form (26). But Bernstein's essays also play on the desire to read for content, to value language chiefly for its ability to communicate a message.

*Content's Dream: Essays 1975–1984* immediately foregrounds the tension between poetic and communicative functions by opening with a Steinian prose poem preface that tries to describe its own experimental form: "hemorrhagic hootenannies, engrossment by engorgement, adjectival remission?" (10). "Such alternatives," the speaker confesses, "can seem more oracular, and exclusionary, than 'straight' talk," and the preface ends with the promise to "tell some tales of terms" in the succeeding discussions (10). Though the essays included in this volume range from academic presentations with formal sentences and paragraphs to the run-on format of talk poetry texts, most follow through on the exegetical promise, and Bernstein even cultivates a tabloid tone of exposé with flashy section headings such as "The Secret of Syntax," "Conspiracies," and "Flesh" that suggest an initiation into the hermeneutic mysteries of the poetry. Bernstein may be skeptical about reifying labels in his poetry, but the paratexts' precise philosophical or clinical terms help to classify information and to temper the difficulty of the poetry he discusses. Like Olson, Bernstein interrupts his essays with numerous parenthetical remarks, though his asides are often concerned with redefining terms in more accessible or strategic ways, such as his translation of a poetic *"techne"* as "practical knowledge, craft, or art" in an effort both to clarify the term and to link aesthetic inquiry to the production of knowledge (354).

His essay personae provide this clarification while insisting on their desire for genuinely open audience participation. In the essay "Blood on the Cutting Room Floor," he valorizes a poem that "keeps beat not to an imposed metrics but to the marks of its own joints and the joints of the reader's projection" (*CD* 362), celebrating the audience as a literary cocreator. At the same time, this paratextual explicator is indeed articulating both an ideal text and the "joints" or components of an appropriate reader response. Given the essay's metaphor of Frankenstein-like language experiments that resist authorial control, this might also be a humorous self-warning on the part of the exegete about possibly monstrous readers who disagree with the creator's own accounts of an experiment.

## Private Acts in Public Places: *Content's Dream*

Bernstein's poetics essays in *Content's Dream* often express an ambivalence about their public impact, oscillating between the use of "I" and "we" in their audience address. Despite the poetry's references to interpellated or decontextualized subjects, Bernstein's essay personae in this volume can slip into a vocabulary of individuality and privacy in describing poetic composition. Though the authorial "I" is not foregrounded to the same degree as in Howe's writing, many of his definitions are made through a first person voice that underscores his reinterpretation of a term: "By vision I mean an engagement of all the senses, and of thought, beyond the readily visible, the statically apparent" (139). In "Thought's Measure," Bernstein defines poetry as a "private act in a public place—the public place being both 'the language'—which is shared by all—and the page, open as it is to reading and rereading (by oneself and others)" (77). In other words, he is not asserting a private experience unmediated by public discourse, but rather a process of defamiliarizing language in order to more fully explore this medium of "social production" (81).[6] A private, antiabsorptive poetry with its ellipses and disjunctions is therefore one of the most highly public acts (82).

But Bernstein's essay personae remain self-conscious about the practical distinction between one's own rereadings of a text and others' interpretations and about circulating pages among a circle of friends instead of a broader audience. The narrators in "Three or Four Things I Know about Him," a piece first published in the little magazine *A Hundred Posters,* argue for a resistant poetry whose focus on language as "the ground of our commonness" can resolve the gap between "our private phantasies & the possibilities of meaningful action" (*CD* 31). Yet their descriptions of a communal "we" become increasingly tentative as they try to define the poet's social responsibilities:

> & obviously we're committed to political struggle, to the necessity of changing current capital distribution, to making the factories & the schools & the hospitals cooperatives, to finding a democracy that allows for the participatory authority of each one to the extent of the responsibility we place on her or him. (30)

The humor in this passage's hyperbole about a participatory democracy whose extent "we" determine emphasizes the limited audience, even among fellow poets, who might endorse both the aspirations and the self-parody. Bernstein's speakers in this essay frequently link discussions of the first person plural to negatives and unreal hypotheses: "As if we didn't already know that 'bad grammar' can speak more truthfully than correct grammar" (29). Behind these rhetorical statements that presuppose an audience's agreement lurks a concern about communicating the poetry's goals; even if a group of like-minded poets organize, how do "we" know that our agendas will not be rejected or mischaracterized by other readers?

Bernstein's concept of a public sphere in *Content's Dream* is never as nightmarish as Spicer's, but his narrators sometimes have difficulty imagining alliances with either mainstream audiences or marginalized social subjects. In the essay "G—/," he transforms the images of disease and criminality that often characterize his disruptive forms in the poetry into a darker portrait of the poet's public:

> we put
> schizophrenics in institutions who offend us we re so easily
> offended    but there is still a sense in which one wants
> to confront to deal with those people who are hurting other
> people being cruel to other people    i mean i dont want
> my friends to be killed    and if someone in my
> community is killing my friends i want to stop them
> and if if you know who is killing my friends i want
> you to tell me who that person is    not so i can put
> them behind bars    but so i can find out whats
> happening with them with us    every murder is a is a
> failure of community    so thats where the need for
> people to testify is    but in our society everything is
> askew
>
> (212)

Though the speaker is intrigued by schizophrenia's power to "offend," he quickly distances himself from that pathology. Contact with an audience is anything but casual here. Not only do the marginal criminals kill the writers, but the all-too-participatory spectators may be complicit in the murder: "if you know who is killing my friends i want / you to tell me." The violence involves a question of semantics, "i mean," as if the act of explication makes the author vulnerable.

To guard against both the potential violence of public exposure and the equally problematic prospect of critical neglect, Bernstein inserts talismanic lists of past and present experimental authors' names in the essays of *Content's Dream* as a way of memorializing the individual poets and their antiabsorptive styles. "The Academy in Peril," originally delivered as part of a 1983 Modern Language Association panel, includes this parenthetical attack on *The Harvard Guide to Contemporary American Writing*:

(Any so-called guide to American poetry that amidst citations of
about 170 poets in its poetry sections (commenting here only on the
older poets in the book's purview—it is even more shameless in the
breadth and blatancy of its omissions among subsequent generations)
that doesn't even *mention* the writing of Stein, Reznikoff, Eigner, or
Mac Low, that merely lists the names of Zukofsky, Oppen, Spicer,
and that hurries over H.D., Loy, and (Riding) Jackson in the same
half-paragraph, while going on to lavish page after page on the usual
suspects, even while extolling Williams, doesn't have a clue about
American literature or Williams.) (248)

Unlike the decontextualization of proper names in the poetry, this remark traces
an entire series of related experimenters from the mention of one name as
Bernstein sweeps away "the usual suspects" and provides a roster of the true avant-
garde poets whodunit in the canon's margins, the real "clue" to twentieth-cen-
tury American literature. The inner parenthetical remark acts as a symbolically
absent center: the contemporary omissions such as Language writers that Bern-
stein's reviews in the "Conspiracies" section of *Content's Dream* redress. These
reviews often use titles with graphic or spatial metaphors, as if attempting to re-
verse each author's invisibility—e. g., "Maintaining Space: Clark Coolidge's Early
Works" or "Making Words Visible / Hannah Weiner." The metaphor of invita-
tion into these specialized spaces that seem both private and public offsets some
of Bernstein's uneasiness about formulaic group identifications that might be-
come an exclusionary "Conspiracy of 'Us'" (343).

## Bernstein's Paratextual Collage: "Artifice of Absorption"

Bernstein continues the lists of marginal authors in his two later essay books, *A
Poetics* and *My Way,* with particular attention to attributing and contextualizing
quotes. The most innovative visual collage of poetic and essay passages in his 1992
text, *A Poetics,* is the eighty-page essay "Artifice of Absorption" that sets off its
multiple quotations in different typefaces. Its cited excerpts are as long as Bern-
stein's commentary, and there are footnotes extensive enough to form a separate
essay. Bernstein begins by contrasting absorptive and antiabsorptive writing, and
he plays with readers' expectations that exegesis requires an absorptive style. But
his goal here is to develop a new critical format in which the limits of exegesis
"are made more audibly / artificial" (*AP* 16) and the criticism adopts poetic de-
vices. Shifting between different genres allows him to experiment with several
versions of the relation between author and audience, negotiating among the
writerly "I," the readerly "you," and "we" together.

To see how the experiment works, one can look first at the questions raised by the "main" essay text. Bernstein lineates his commentary as a free verse poem although many of the sentences would fit within paragraphs of a conventional persuasive essay. "Artifice" is an open challenge to readers who prefer Language prose essays to the poetry, asking them to evaluate what form or function distinguishes the two genres. Bernstein provides the following overview, for example, of poetry by Clark Coolidge:

Clark Coolidge's improvisatory extensions
of the line refuse the closure of the subject/verb/object
sentence; refuse, that is, the syntactic ideality
of the complete sentence, in which each part
of speech operates in its definable place so that
a grammatic paradigm is superimposed on the actual
unfolding of the semantic strings.

(AP 60)

By using such dense language in this passage, Bernstein refutes the premise that an explanatory review will be inherently easier to absorb than an elliptical poem, and he also pointedly makes the description of a normative sentence the most abstract part of the passage. It's more difficult to assess the impact of the poetic lineation. He self-consciously uses line breaks (e.g., "extensions / of the line") to visually represent Coolidge's own extended lines and deferred syntax, but the departure from a prose essay format may also make the text more impermeable for readers. Such ambiguities reinforce the point that absorptive or antiabsorptive styles are relative terms determined by the syntactical patterns that a reader has seen most frequently.

Taking an entire page of "Artifice" as a unit reveals a more complex layering of poetic and prose formats. There are seven different enclosed or ongoing texts in Bernstein's discussion of Bob Perelman's writings on page 33, each with another perspective on the relation between author and reader (see fig. 5.1). Perelman's terse poetry lines at the top, left over from a longer quote on the previous page, present the image of writer and reader held together only by their assumption of a common "language glue" as they try to decipher a text "in the dark" (33). That tenuous connection is further undermined by Perelman's lecture comment about American news media constructions of "'us,'" an imposed consensus that prevents a participatory experience of reading. As if to reflect this one-way communication, there is little semantic play in Perelman's own prose commentary. The description of a public language shifts once again in the third Perelman quote, taken from another poem, moving from metaphors of darkness to vision and revision. This citation represents the writer and reader confronting each other through a glass partition misted by their breath. The mist created by the close

alone in the dark
big wide streets lined with language glue

Perelman comments:

> The reader and the writer, "the you and the I," are such languages
> transforming into pulp language, non-languages and back, de-
> graded, exploded, overburdened systems of public & private ad-
> dress. There's no inner escape from our environment, where such
> powerful emblems of coercion as USA TODAY constantly conflate the
> initials U.S. with their editorial staff and with "us," so that "we"
> read that "we" are buoyed by the progress of the Salvadoran army
> or that "we" are attending more ballgames than ever this summer.[16]

Or, as he writes in "Binary": "Finally the I
writing / and the you reading (breath still misting
the glass) / examples of the body partitioned by the
word" [*The First World*, p. 47].

Absorption is blocked by misting
this glass, or by breaking it, or
by painting on its surface. Any

16. Bob Perelman, "Notes on *The First World*", *Line* 6 (1985), 101, 108–109;
this talk was originally presented at the New Poetics Colloquium in Vancouver. The
poems quoted by Perelman in his talk, as well as the citations that follow, are from
*The First World* (Great Barrington, Mass.: The Figures, 1986). —"If only the plot
would leave people alone", Perelman writes in "Anti-Oedipus" (p. 20). His passion-
ate refusal to be housed by the poem, his insistence on breaking loose from the social
hypnosis that deadens response, nonetheless cannot readily be understood as prevent-
ing absorption, despite its striking awareness of itself as a poetry & its forthright
address to the reader. For Perelman has created poetry that is funny, political, engag-
ing—and does not distance itself from the reader in ways we have grown accustomed
to. In a recent interview Perelman was careful to put off the suggestion that because
his poems do not employ causal unity (are not "little short stories"), they are there-
fore not coherent. "China", a work in *The First World*, "coheres grammatically,
thematically, politically in terms of tone. It's certainly not something that throws you
off the track, like playing trains as a kid, whipping from side to side until someone
falls off—it's not that." This last image of a train flipping the tracks is precisely a
description of the effect of the antiabsorptive on reading. Interview by George Hart-
ley, conducted in Berkeley in 1986, quoted in "Jameson's Perelman: Reification and
the Material Signifier", a draft chapter of Hartley's dissertation (University of New
Mexico); not included in the chapter of the same name in Hartley's *Textual Politics
of the Language Poets* (Bloomington: Indiana University Press, 1989).

Fig. 5.1. Excerpt from Charles Bernstein, "Artifice of Absorption," *A Poetics*, p.33. Copy-
right 1992 by Charles Bernstein. Reprinted by permission of Charles Bernstein.

contact between author and audience, as Bernstein suggests in his own commentary about absorption, is not obscuring but revealing, a symbol for language that is no longer taken for granted as a transparent means of conveying a message.

Which description of the relation between writer and audience is the authoritative one here? Does an author's commentary or poetry carry more weight, and if the latter, which poetic excerpt should one choose? Bernstein provides no transitions between passages beyond a neutral conjunction such as "Or." Readers approaching the page as a linear progression may want to see the misted glass image as a compromise or synthesis that depicts language both as an intimate exchange and a barrier. They may be puzzled, however, by the final twist in Bernstein's small print note that takes up nearly half this page. He argues that Perelman's poetry does not really prevent absorption, despite its consciousness of its own artifice, because it manages to be "funny, political, engaging" and "does not distance itself from the reader in ways we have grown accustomed to" (*AP* 33).

Like a parody of Perelman's editorial boards that impose their consensus on readers, this last-minute judgment makes the reader interrogate the identity of the "we" who have grown accustomed to certain definitions of absorptive or impermeable texts. It might signify Language writers; the exchanges on this page occur among the poets and their critics. It might also designate readers who are put off by the Language label or by any innovative format without looking to see what an individual text offers. What would it mean to break the glass between author and reader as Bernstein expresses it, bracketing this page with our own collaborative contribution to the dialogues between the poetry excerpts and paratexts? In this respect, "Artifice of Absorption" serves the paradigmatic function of a paratext, issuing an invitation to the readers to respond to its word games with their own inventions.

The nature of "Artifice"'s invitation, however, has changed from that in many of the *Content's Dream* essays, just as the status of Language poetry itself changed over the eighties and nineties, with increased scholarly attention to the movement and a number of the writers now holding academic positions as literature professors. This does not necessarily mark the co-optation of a poetic revolution, but it has prompted different narrative frames for Language history. The passage from Bernstein's MLA piece on Williams provides authors' names from overlooked poetic genealogies to be recovered. Bernstein's shifting images of writer and reader in "Artifice" still manifest concern over who reads Language poetry carefully, but the result of the essay's extensive intertextuality is less a portrait of isolated avant-gardes against a canon than of a recognized revolutionary tradition whose contributors can discuss their relation to numerous experimental predecessors and counterparts. While a few critics who favor "mimetic" writing (*AP* 42) are permanently exiled from Bernstein's literary community, he nevertheless expands the discussion of Language poetry by comparing its techniques to widely diverse written and aural experiments across countries and time periods: Emily Dickinson's unconventional punctuation, Hugh MacDiarmid's Scots poetry, Velimir Khlebnikov's *zaum* writing, e. e. cummings's typography, John Coltrane's music, and shamanistic rituals. Some of his footnotes even reclaim absorptive writers for antiabsorptive projects. Bernstein includes a quote from Ford Madox Ford that advocates a transparent writing style, but then observes in a note that Ford's "wonderfully digressive and ornately self-conscious" opening remarks to the reader violate his own compositional rules (28). It seems fitting to the expansive margins of this revolutionary tradition that a writer whose "central" text rejects its practices is admitted in a note because of his own paratextual preface.

## Dialects, Ideolects, and Translations: Explicating *My Way*

Does the collage of styles and the incorporation of varied past and present names strengthen an oppositional poetry or simply create a new canon? The tension that Perelman notes between disrupting all characterization and stating the value of specific writers in *A Poetics* is even more pronounced in Bernstein's 1999 volume *My Way.*[7] This selection of essays and poems foregrounds Bernstein's conflicting desires to reflect the fluid, idiosyncratic nature of individual language experiments and to characterize them as part of broader communal practices in order to explain the significance of the experiments to an audience.

The essay "Poetics of the Americas" in *My Way,* for example, contextualizes Language poetry by citing other nonstandard private, regional, and group language practices, although he describes them as "heterogeneous and anomalous elements" rather than fixed devices (114). Originally published as an article in *Modernism/Modernity,* this essay recalls Olson's celebration of multiple, intersecting language communities in the ideal polis:

> The cultural space of this impossible America is not carved up by national borders or language borders but transected by innumerable overlaying, contradictory or polydictory, traditions and proclivities and histories and regions and peoples and circumstances and identities and families and collectivities and dissolutions—dialects and ideolects not National Tongues, localities and habitations not States. (113)

Bernstein is more willing than Olson to concede that the nation he builds in his paratexts may be a series of "impossible" constructs—"Imagination[s]" or "'Image Nations'" as he echoes Robin Blaser (136). The passage above, held together loosely by conjunctions and sound patterns, creates the impression of an excess of potentially contested categories rather than one inclusive state.

But is Bernstein's emphasis on multiple language practices genuinely different from the identity politics he critiques? It is telling that he has to redefine many of the terms he borrows, bringing several theoretical frameworks into "con-VERSation" (*MW* 121) if not complete agreement. He discusses dialect poetry, in Edward Brathwaite's sense of "'the *submerged* area of dialect'" as a *"nation language"'* based on a shared diaspora history (120), but Bernstein argues that contemporary forms of dialect poetry may be moving toward a "dialectical" literature that is less nationalistic: it "refuses allegiance to Standard English without necessarily basing its claim on an affiliation with a definable group's speaking practice" (117).[8] Rather than explain in detail the process of that dialectical transition away from a fixed group identity, however, Bernstein refocuses his attention on the language experiments of an "ideolectical" writing (117). He coins this term by redefining *idiolect,* an individual's unique speech style, as an "ideologically informed nonstandard language practice" (117). Bernstein seems to model the ideolectical technique here with his own strategic word transformations. The ideolect becomes the perfect version of a unique poetics, "a rejection or troubling of identity structures, group or individual" as static characterizations (134) that nevertheless closely reveals the poet's "process of thinking" (117).

Bernstein's preference for ideolectical parts that elude totalizing definitions corresponds to his ongoing efforts to chart a creative collage style for paratexts. Structurally, *My Way* extends the collage of "Artifice" to the unit of the book, offering a selection of poems, essays, interviews, and speeches that is even more diverse than the stylistic range of his previous essay volumes. Individual essays incorporate brief poems or mimic aspects of his poetic language in their own sentences. "Is prose justified? Or aren't you the kind that tells? That's no prose that's my default. Default is in our sorrow not our swells" (47). This excerpt from "What's Art Got to Do with It?" carries out Bernstein's challenge to rigid academic prose; despite the paragraph format, the sentences with their mangled maxims and internal rhyme might have come directly from one of Bernstein's poetry texts. As for readerly address, the seductive evasions and twists in this essay passage recall Spicer's mock commentaries.

Yet conventional exegesis is still an integral part of Bernstein's collages in *My Way.* When the essay "The Revenge of the Poet-Critic," for example, mixes Dr. Seuss–style lyrics among its paragraphs, it only intensifies the contrast between the pared-down sound play of the poetry (e.g., "There's flotsam in my jetsam" [10] or "Don't Be So Sure / *[Don't Be Saussure]*" [5]) and the definitions, examples, and logical transitions in other parts of the commentary as he debates the social "politics of poetic form" (4). One can read the volume as a series of narratorial asides to the reader, testing out various absorptive and antiabsorptive techniques in both prose and poetry to communicate his points.

The very premise of an ideolect, arguably, necessitates some complementary exegesis about the author's project. The ultimate ideolect becomes incomprehensible to anyone but the writer, a point that Bernstein concedes in "Poetics of the Americas" when he describes the Australian author Javant Biarujia inventing his own "Taneraic" language and writing poetry in it. The experiment intrigues Bernstein, and yet such writing requires the paratextual translations and dictionary entries that Biarujia also publishes in order to create an audience beyond the few readers who would enjoy the poetry for the sound alone. It's suggestive that semantic and orthographic accuracy matter in Bernstein's own discussion of this poet; while Spicer declares in *After Lorca* that the translator is always right, Bernstein reassures readers that he's presenting the material accurately, stating that he submitted an early draft of the essay to Biarujia so that the poet might respond to the analysis and correct the Taneraic spellings (*MW* 135).

The reader's need for directions or definitions for an ideolectical poetry is the subject of Bernstein's "A Test of Poetry," a piece in *My Way* composed of questions that he received from a Chinese translator of his poems. Demanding word-by-word explication and cultural contexts—"But who is Uncle Hodgepodge? / And what does *familiar freight* / *to the returning antelope* mean?" (53)—the translator tries to order the unfamiliar freight of a hodgepodge Language text into literal scenarios with accessible subjects, settings, and emotional conflicts. Bernstein's inclusion of these questions offers a critique of stock criteria for a literary text; the translator is missing the point of the original poem's multivalent language play. The irony, however, immediately creates outsider and insider distinctions based on one's familiarity with Bernstein's paratexts. If the reader gets the joke, relishing Bernstein's transformation of the translator's questions into a new Language poem, it is precisely because he or she is not a "witless witness" (54) but has learned the appropriate participatory response to a disruptive poetry after having absorbed the essays on poetic method.

## "To Come to Terms with Error": Bernstein and Pound

Bernstein's determination to provide necessary paratextual explanations for readers without imposing too much interpretive closure on the poetry explains why Ezra Pound remains such a problematic figure in his compositions: here, as for Olson, is a stylistic precursor who tried to articulate the structural and political coherence of his disjunctive epic in authoritative essays. Bernstein acknowledges the literary influence of Pound's poetry on Language writing but returns to the controversy over Pound's essays and broadcasts. Although Pound's statements are not as formally creative as the paratexts of later authors, Bernstein sees in Pound's writing the conflicts of the paratextual poet trying to constitute an audience. Interpreting the connection between Pound's poetry and paratexts becomes crucial to Bernstein's own sense of communal identity as an experimental poet.

Bernstein's essays present different views of that connection, but perhaps the most striking is the series of extraordinary mixed metaphors in "Pounding Fascism" in *A Poetics* where he speculates that the innovation of Pound's poetry may have *caused* his attraction to totalizing systems:

> There is a price to be paid for poetry; its practice can poison as fatally as sniffing glue or inhaling coal dust. Madame Curie did not know about the lethal aftereffects of invisible radiation when she conducted her experiments; we know from her experience that there are risks that cannot be prevented until after the first victims have made the effects visible. Is cultural megalomania a symptom of being overwhelmed by the incommensurable and intractable autonomy of fragments, that will not submit to a unitary measure, hierarchically predetermined . . . ? (*AP* 122)

Here it is not the reader but the poet himself who requires clarity and coherence after the radical indeterminacy of an avant-garde composition. Bernstein first associates the poetry with unsafe labor conditions and substance abuse before settling on the image of a scientific discovery made at high risk. In this context, "price" is a significant analogy. Bernstein suggests that the totalizing statements of poetics and politics may have been a necessary response—less for Pound than for his readers and successors, since the paratexts provided a warning both about the difficulties of the poetry and the hazards of trying to resolve that difficulty too easily or of extrapolating from one's own political poetics to a restructured polis. For Bernstein, Pound's greatest triumph ironically becomes his failure to resolve the gap between his doctrines and his poetry, as the polyphony of the sources, dialects, and allusions of *The Cantos* negates his attempts to impose order. The authoritarian statements within and outside the poem become one component among many disparate elements, a "debased material" that can be "framed and denounced by those readers able to pick and choose for themselves" (125).

Having demonstrated the pitfalls for the avant-gardist, Pound becomes a kind of antiguide whose statements Bernstein distorts in order to map out alternative paratextual strategies of public address. He opens his *My Way* essay "Pound and the Poetry of Today" with a parody of Pound's radio broadcasts: "This is Charles Bernstein speaking . . . from the Upper West Side of Manhattan, home of Zabar's and Barney Greengrass, the Sturgeon King" (155), contrasting his local place markers and light tone with the bombastic claims of the Rome broadcasts. He avoids delineating a fixed cultural or poetic identity for himself; rather he defines himself through an ongoing process of debate and word play. The essay is headed by an anti-Semitic Pound quotation as epigraph: "'What Greek logomachy had in common with the Hebrew poison was debate, dialectic, sophistry, the critical activity that destroys faith . . .'" (155). Bernstein seizes upon the statement, transforming Jewishness from an ethnic identity into a conscious act of critical interrogation of any totalizing faith. He links that critical activity to broad-ranging paratextual debates with other poets or scholars about "what they/we cannot understand" in Pound's fascist pronouncements (155), their shared queries exposing the ways in which the "lacunas in Pound's guides to culture have begun to speak" (162).

If Pound's unintentional legacy is the contradictions and limitations in his writing, Bernstein increasingly incorporates a sense of the restrictions of specific audience addresses in both his poetry and paratexts. Behind the experimentation with different genres in the essays are pragmatic discussions about the self-perpetuating quality of the formats. Who comes to poetry reading series and why, or what happens to the doctoral student who ignores audience expectations for an academic monograph? Bernstein inserts his own fake or misappropriated publicity blurbs in the poetry itself to satirize literary marketing. *Dark City* features a number of such reviews spliced together from different sources, some with exaggerated boasts that poke fun at overly ambitious political claims for a text: "All Americans who care about their country's place in the world will find this book worth reading" (96). Other "review" passages in the poems make a mockery of absorptive clarity:

> Bernstein's argument is an important one and his discussion is consistently thoughtful, energetic, and smoothly handled. Any reader of the modern verse epic will find *The Tale of the Tribe: Ezra Pound and the Modern Verse Epic* stimulating and provocative. (92)

This blurb is nearly information free with its nondescript adjectives and an audience recommendation copied from the book's title. That this decontextualized review in fact concerns the work of critic Michael André Bernstein (the full name is never specified) rather than poet Charles gently undercuts the poet's earlier insistence on the importance of publicizing authors' names. The Pound allusion works as a double-edged reference, inviting us to assess Pound's distinctive style against the banal pronouncements here and also to compare the modernist's attempts at creating communal narratives with the advertising tools designed to erase difference in selling books to as broad an audience as possible.

Between reading guides that lack any standard of quality beyond their marketability and modernist essays that would fix their tales of a tribe too dogmatically, where does Bernstein place his own paratexts and their demands upon an audience? The localized Manhattan neighborhood to which he invites readers in "Pound and the Poetry of Today" becomes a fictive construct in "Warning—Poetry Area: Publics under Construction" when he laments that "we can only imagine the public square, the town green, a Central Park of our poetries, where . . . we might jostle against one another" (*MW* 311). This town space, he envisions, can be provided partly by media such as public radio, though he reiterates that neither old technologies nor Internet resources will provide a forum for poetry without readers' efforts to become culturally informed. At other points, Bernstein implies that a broad public is not necessarily the target audience for an avant-garde performance. In "Close Listening," Bernstein discusses the social function of poetry readings, concluding that the poet's most productive exchanges are with an "audience of peers" rather than a general public or students (*MW* 301), although the scholarly essay format of the writing is clearly intended for some of those students.

Since Bernstein's paratexts were originally presented in contexts ranging from national academic conferences to small Language poetry forums, it might be easy to account for the diversity of their arguments and audience addresses. But their stylistic range involves more than changes in presentation venue. Bernstein tests out different paratextual formats for fear of becoming trapped in a single one, and he also delights in the "unbridgeable lacuna" (*AP* 12) between his own desire to explicate a text and its resistance to such summation. Ultimately Bernstein is less interested in the assimilation of poetry and criticism than in the differences that are not resolved between them: an author's insistence on accurate translations juxtaposed with models of "surplus explanation" and errors (168), or the specter of an essay begun as "playful considerations of possibility" (162) that may quickly become a statement of authority to its readers (161). By promising, "I've only just begun to contradict myself" (*MW* 97), without recourse to Whitman's rhetoric of containment, he acknowledges the complexity of crafting a resistant writing that does not reinscribe old discourses of power.

Bernstein, I have argued, creates essays that are simultaneously more straightforward and less trustworthy than those of Olson or Howe; he offers helpful summations that he won't fully endorse in a lucid argumentative style he won't entirely discard. If readers feel overwhelmed by the author's toll-taking shifts in language, Bernstein insists that they create their own compensations. The disjunctions among an ideolectical poetry, its paratextual translations, and the author's retractions, he asserts, are what allow a text to become something other than its initial "frame lock" of style or argument (*MW* 90). A reader may disagree with individual forms and premises but will frequently find it hard not to share Bernstein's pleasure in getting "lost somewhere between the sentences / right in the middle of the verses" (190) that comprise his poetry-paratext combinations. The trip is circuitous not because he withholds answers but because his continually revised sets of directions ask readers to reformulate the questions they began with about the interpretation of an avant-garde poetry.

# 6

## Illustrated Histories: The Paratextual Narratives of Lorenzo Thomas and Johanna Drucker

My study thus far has examined the increasing reliance of an American avant-garde poetry on paratexts, analyzing the development of these forms from essays and parenthetical asides to components in prose-poetic texts and palimpsests. I would like to expand the discussion of paratextual poetry by looking at two contemporary authors whose books recall the early avant-gardists' fascination with popular culture formats. Neither author offers a set definition of a public poetry. They adapt popular formats and mass media images in their paratexts precisely to underscore the difficulty of making communal claims; they echo Spicer's ambivalence about public exposure and the Language poets' protest against commodified advertising language. Yet the two authors continue to make paratextual dialogues a central part of their compositions as a way of investigating the politics of different models of reader participation.

The palimpsest genre, I have argued, creates its own revolution-within-tradition through the contrast between a familiar paratext and the poet's revisions. What could be more easily assimilated by a broad audience than the sensationalist plots of classic horror movies? Lorenzo Thomas inserts stills from movies of gothic evildoers menacing the heroes' neighborhoods in his books, the pictures and their story lines framing his ironic poetic commentaries on national paranoia, racial conflicts, and readers who are trained as passive spectators.

Johanna Drucker, in her two artist's books published in 1990, also works with widely familiar genres, creating paratextual narratives modeled on children's history books and pulp biographies. These books take the premise of the Spicerian mistranslation or the palimpsest one step further. Spicer in *After Lorca* turns his predecessor's writing into a ghostly text to be revised and even invents source poems written in an imitation of Lorca's style. Drucker simplifies that process by inventing all her own source documents, fake histories that openly acknowledge their limitations and biases to suggest new forms of communal historiography.

It is no coincidence that both Drucker and Thomas foreground visual mass media icons in these text-paratext dialogues. Their poetry deconstructs the clichés of conformists versus grotesque outsiders suggested by the decontextualized images. But the play with images and diagrams that fail to explicate their accompanying texts also captures the basic tension within the paratext form, a seemingly explanatory document that in fact augments, revises, or even contradicts the poetic text. As in the text-paratext relations I discuss with previous authors, the readers can scrutinize each poet's argument about a participatory art when they absorb the background in the paratextual sources, as well as the disjunctions between poetry and paratext.

## Framed Performances: Lorenzo Thomas's American Gothic

Lorenzo Thomas's illustrated histories are based on sharp formal distinctions between poetry and source paratext. While Howe often defends subjects reductively characterized as monstrous or marginal in her sources, Thomas's horror film paratexts feature actual screen monsters as the symbolic preface for his history lessons couched in poetic collages of citations and conversational fragments. Thomas does not easily fit critical categories with this blend of social critique, high modernist formats, and postmodernist camp, techniques that reflect his mistrust of essentializing identity politics. He draws eclectically from a range of predecessors: Ezra Pound, Robert Frost, Langston Hughes, Melvin Tolson, Aimé Césaire, Léon Damas, and Roberto McKay. In the early sixties, Thomas was one of the youngest members of the New York Umbra workshop, a circle of African American poets that included Ishmael Reed and Calvin Hernton and that had ties to other local and international avant-garde poetry, as well as to the beginning of Black Arts writing. Yet he remains outside the purview of most scholarship on contemporary American experimental poetry.[1]

To answer the question of why he uses movie paratexts in his first two poetry collections, one can begin with the cover of his 1981 book *The Bathers*.[2] Its Duchamp-like collage superimposes cutouts of modern luxury goods on a Renoir painting of bathing nudes (see fig. 6.1). The collage suggestively places Thomas's use of film paratexts in an avant-garde tradition of ironically framed ready-mades and icons. Looking only at the cover, readers might expect either a poetic tribute to Dada or perhaps a discussion in Bürger's vein about the commodification of the avant-garde. What we find instead is that the "Bathers" in Thomas's title poem are civil rights marchers in Birmingham in 1963 who were attacked by police with water hoses and dogs (see fig. 6.2). The juxtaposition immediately raises questions about Thomas's project that do not usually come up in a Dada text. What relation can there be between a poet adapting an aesthetic style within a primarily white experimental tradition and the protesters flung against a wall with little choice about strategies of resistance? When there are enough real-life monsters, moreover, and when the widely televised images of the Birmingham police brutality changed viewers' attitudes towards the protesters, why would a poet eschew realist portraits for an elaborate deconstruction of monster movie paratexts?

Thomas's response is best summed up by one of his narrators who watches a newsreel of post–World War II American politics and wails that "we was framed!" (*B* 131)—surely a unique response among the praises or condemnations of United States policy. The danger, he implies more seriously, is indeed that we were visually framed: the newsreel images of embattled civil rights protesters, atomic explosions, and Vietnam-bound troops have become stock postwar icons in a way that radically diminishes their original impact. In contrast, Thomas translates racial violence into an analysis of a horror movie's "wraiths of aberration on the screen / All black & white" (*C* 103) in order to strip away the verbal and visual devices that allow an audience to consume easy narratives of villains or heroes.

The movie paratexts enter Thomas's books through publicity stills and sketches of black zombies, black-caped vampires, and shadowy invisible men in dark glasses—a whole repertoire of film clichés in which darkness is synonymous with evil and must be defeated. His poetic narrators play on these stereotypes, teas-

Fig. 6.1. Cover collage from Lorenzo Thomas, *The Bathers*. Artwork by Cecilio Thomas. Courtesy of Lorenzo Thomas, Cecilio Thomas, and I. Reed Books.

Fig. 6.2. Title page from Lorenzo Thomas, *The Bathers*. Artwork by Cecilio Thomas. Courtesy of Lorenzo Thomas, Cecilio Thomas, and I. Reed Books.

ing readers with titles like "I Just Want To Reach Out And Bite You Baby" (*B* 57) or "Serpent Guerillas" (119). The movies' popcorn monsters and invading aliens, Thomas suggests in a series of imaginative metaphors in his essay "Big House Movies," evoke historical skeletons in domestic American closets as they substitute for a vanished servant class, offering post-Reconstruction audiences new fantasies of alternately entertaining and threatening Others. "[G]ood help," the narrator quips dryly, "is so hard to find. So God invented the movies" (*C* 89).

Thomas's own poetic inventions are the opposite of labor-saving devices. Because he knows that audiences are probably more familiar with the sensational promotional stills rather than with specific movie plots, he juxtaposes each still with a series of poetic responses that bring out the conflicts over definitions of communal identity embedded in the film narratives. The reader not only has to retrieve the paratextual source but has to analyze it along with the multiple intertexts in Thomas's verbal play that subvert the clichés of darkness and light the stills initially suggest.

The first gothic paratext in his 1979 poetry collection, *Chances are Few,* is the Universal Pictures version of *The Invisible Man.* Thomas includes a still from the 1933 film of Claude Rains's darkly shadowed and bandaged protagonist (see fig. 6.3). The character has erased all pigmentation from his body, a surface change that unexpectedly transforms him into a sociopath who murders the townspeople and thus justifies the violence that they must use against him. His monstrousness seems as evident as the open record of his experiment now spread in front of him. Thomas rereads this paratextual still by juxtaposing it with song lyrics from blues performer Percy Mayfield. The blues lyrics about never having received an even break from anyone but God parody the film's idea of community justice and move the questions about skin color and ostracism into an explicitly racialized context. It is characteristic of Thomas's reversals of dark gothic imagery that most of the shadowy villains he selects are actually white; the Invisible Man's countenance is metaphorically exposed as a blank white space on the facing page. With his hands covering his ears, Rains seems to be shutting out the incongruous blues music intruding in the lower margins.

The intertext that Thomas evokes with this blues quote is of course Ralph Ellison's 1952 novel. Ellison rewrote Wells's mad scientist, who dreams of creating a new race to terrorize the world, as a black protagonist whose social invisibility is forced upon him by a white community that acknowledges neither the history of injustice nor the present danger that he represents. "'*What did I do,*'" Ellison's narrator echoes a Louis Armstrong lyric, "'*To be so black / And blue?*'" (12). Both Ellison and Thomas emphasize the constructedness of a "black" identity in order to ask whether subjects can rewrite the social roles they have been assigned. A quarter century after Ellison's narrator declares that he is neither a "spook" nor "one of your Hollywood-movie ectoplasms" (3), Thomas satirizes both black and white characters who remain as two-dimensional as the specters in his paratextual stills. Many of the subjects in *Chances are Few* have no "Personal Anthropology" (22) to decode because they are too possessed, in the gothic sense, by the televisions and movie houses that provide them with fictions of identity. "America designs / Ourselves" as "Projections in the dark" that have become as flatly familiar as "wallpaper," the narrator asserts in the sardonically titled "Class Action" (105). The question that Thomas poses in "Screen Test" is not "why does popular America persist in death dreams?" (95) but whether these "Pictures of pictures" (95) leave any space for resistance when every rebellious gesture freezes into a picturesque pose and the would-be artist remains "poised, / On the threshold of cleverer interpretations," mesmerized by the latest on-screen plot twist (100) without recognizing his own absorption.

To disrupt the recycled stereotypes behind these two-dimensional subjects, Thomas follows *The Invisible Man* paratext with a deliberately provocative in-

No one
has ever
given me
an even break
but God

—*Percy Mayfield*

Fig. 6.3. Excerpts from Lorenzo Thomas, *Chances are Few*, pp. 42 and 43. Film still copyright 2001 by Universal City Studios, Inc. Courtesy of Universal Studios Publishing Rights. All rights reserved.

terracial tableau from a less familiar late night movie. Let the reader beware who jumps to conclusions about the 1956 RKO film *I Walked with a Zombie* based on the promotional still of a tall, half-clothed black man carrying an unconscious white woman (see fig. 6.4). The whimsical blues quote on the following page, "'You know, life is just a puzzle. . . .'" (*C* 77), and the subtle echo of Ellison's description of *whites* as dangerous sleepwalkers are the sole clues that this still, designed to play on a white audience's fear of miscegenation, completely misrepresents the monsters in the movie plot.

Only the reader who goes beyond the picture to retrieve the paratextual source will get the irony: the voodoo guard shown in this still is never more than an ominous background presence, while the woman he carries is the evil zombie of the movie's title. Her earlier sleepwalking existence and now her death are punishment for the allegorical crime of setting brother against brother within the island's ruling white family, the planters whose ancestors brought slaves to the West Indian settlement. The younger brother's fraternal rebellion develops alongside the islanders' more covert challenges to white authority through performance and song lyrics. Not only are whites induced to participate in voodoo rituals, but a calypso musician sings openly about the scandals in the white family while pretending that he doesn't know the brothers are present. Through these performances, the whites are assigned the role that Ellison associated with a black community, a group treated as both invisible and notorious.

Thomas uses this atypical zombie movie paratext with its disruptive performances to introduce a poetry section entitled "The Marvelous Land of Indefinitions" (*C* 78). The title comes from his translation of a poem by Panamanian author Roberto McKay that criticizes political writers who prefer aesthetic games to action on behalf of the common people they valorize. Throughout *Chances are Few,* Thomas suggests strategic indefinitions as a more complex political tool that interrogates the fiction of a reified popular language or racial identity. His text-paratext juxtapositions, for example, mix dramatic dialogue, poetic diction, regional slang, black English dialects, creative translations, and calypso and reggae lyrics.[3] Where Bernstein might extrapolate an impossible nation from these language communities, Thomas's narrators maintain a stronger tone of self-parody, using rapid shifts in speech patterns like defensive feints to keep themselves from being linked to any one characterization. "Can I mention 'Round Midnight' here / As she reads me the Bible?" one of his narrators wonders about a screen idol as his romantic "posings just shuffle along" (96). Thomas's loose translation of the French Guianan poet Léon Damas erupts into modern American jazz sessions and Hollywood kung-fu fight scenes like a campy collage of "History lessons in a minor scale" (64). Which movie plot or expression, Thomas asks rhetorically, represents an authentic black identity?

Fig. 6.4. Excerpt from Lorenzo Thomas, *Chances are Few,* p. 76. Film still from *I Walked with a Zombie* © 1956 RKO Pictures. All rights reserved.

Thomas suggests that these indefinitions, however difficult to chart, are the only alternative to characterizations whose easy absorption by viewers masks the violence of that consumption process. In *Dracula,* one of his most intricate gothic paratextual poems, he literalizes the motif of parasitic consumption. First published as a chapbook in 1973 and then reprinted in *The Bathers,* the poem shifts between an outsider's address to "you" and a celebration of "our" movie monster by viewers unwilling to probe the stock roles and forcible erasures in their own histories. The result is a caricature that repeats itself endlessly; *Dracula* pays tribute to the "Worst film of 1932 1958 and," the narrator warns, "Unless we get wise to our- / Selves next year over again" (*B* 44). Thomas's monster is once again white, this time an immigrant success story. Britt Wilkie's sketches, reproduced from the original chapbook, fuse famous screen vampires with Thomas's modernized "American / Dracula" (48) who metamorphoses from a foreigner with antiquated costumes into a blankly featureless business traveler (see fig. 6.5).[4] The black capes and overcoats in the sketches heighten the starkness of the monster's pallor and its symbolism in Thomas's poem as a pun on white America's lack of self-reflection or soul: "that thing we no longer discover / Effective about our own faces in the glass" (45). Thomas's specter keeps nothing of Bela Lugosi's mystique, Christopher Lee's seductiveness, or even Max Schreck's silent menace; the new Dracula is a banal and over-publicized "WORK OF ART no matter how / Unnecessary it remain to our flesh" (46).

In contrast to this "Unnecessary" creation, both the vampire and the "dull artist" who invents him "lus[t]" for an "unwanted" but "necessary" blackness (*B* 46, 47): a fetishized African American art, music, and even blood to counteract the decay of their aesthetics. In a rapid montage of story fragments, the "Suspended sentences" (46) of the vampire story are overheard and completed by a lynch mob whose desire to assimilate or consume that black presence turns murderous. The crucifixes from which the film vampires recoil are proudly adopted by the American Dracula in scenes reminiscent of Klan crosses and hangings; the poem was originally written after Klan shootings in Selma. The narrator's descriptions of these attacks as "the holy mystery of / Our people in this country today" (46–47), with "cities serving the sacrament negro" (47), expose the extent of the crowds' dependence upon the victims they hate, the "Suspended sentences" perversely recalling the Christ imagery in Melville's *Billy Budd, Sailor,* whose protagonist is also sacrificed to maintain communal order: "O, 'tis me, not the sentence they'll suspend" (*BB* 132). The poet implicitly contrasts his creative revisions of these canonical and popular texts with the "dying" music of the contemporary white plagiarists who are "tired of our thoughtful survival" (*B* 47) but cannot see any flaws in their scapegoat rhetoric or the possibility of alternative narratives. The narrator concedes that "it is a sense of loss / We lack" (47).

## Hollywood After-Images and Power Blackouts

Thomas's poetry-paratext juxtapositions restore those moments of loss and displacement, the structural "HICCUP!!!" (*C* 66) when any system of communal representation is betrayed as an artificial construct. The blank white space facing the Invisible Man in *Chances are Few,* for example, becomes a metaphoric power blackout by the end of the volume. The prose piece "Hat Red" superimposes alien invasion movie plots on memories of an actual New York City blackout, a text that is pointedly not illustrated by any visual still or sketch. Instead of incomprehensible monsters, it is the aliens who are now baffled by our communal signals: "The UFOs hung calmly in the velvet pitch above the dimmed skyline, their radios monitoring unintelligible broadcasts of Lyndon Johnson's unintelligible Texas drawl" (112).

Fig. 6.5. Sketch by Britton Wilkie from Lorenzo Thomas, *The Bathers,* p. 41. Courtesy of Lorenzo Thomas and I. Reed Books.

The narrator's assertions of truth-value and transparency falter in his attempt to record an image of this loss of imagery:

> I'm so breathless because this is too true. And it's still true today. It did happen for true and I saw it. Or did not see it, that is, I mean in the darkness. And there is a many true words in this story of that day that *was* a night in New York City. Some of the holy ones are articles and verbs nouns and so forth. It was a sign from greater powers than we be and, so sadly, few of we on earth have heed the signals hidden there and then in that dark. (*C* 115)

Whereas the movies metaphorically project light into darkness to convey their message, Thomas's blackout passage "mean[s] in the darkness" by focusing on signs that are paradoxically "too true," conventions of syntax, diction, and rhetoric that break down to mark the failure of a shared community; even the suggestion of a stable speaking presence in "breathless" is distanced by the passage of time asserted in "it's still true today." Binaries collapse, not only day and night but past and present, singular and plural, subject and object, standardized English and dialect. Without its old semantic signposts, the blacked-out city becomes an ongoing argument about permeable national borders with "Brother against brother" (*C* 114), threats of Viet Cong invasions, and demonic apparitions—a wild proliferation of conspiracy plots that the speaker can do nothing to sort out or assuage.

Such confusion, Thomas's narrators admit, is not likely to promote an author's popularity. As the speaker explains ruefully in "Class Action": "I'm a lie! Because I see in twos or threes, / Because my view is amplified by night" rather than simplified to a reductive clarity (*C* 110). Thomas often betrays impatience with the premise of finding a poetry in "our common speech" (*B* 141) or with attempts to read a poem as a transparent political message.[5] His answer to Ellison's unwakable social sleepwalkers is to exhort his own black or white performers to "Sleep lightly in American accents" (*C* 91), where any communal allegiance is approached as an accented foreign language that cannot fully characterize its speakers. He creates narratives of ancient African spirits complaining about their reincarnation in American safari films, or imagines a fellow poet caught in the same recycled plots that confront his characters: "When Dukardo Boarded the Astro-Jet, He Already Done Seen the Movie" (82). If Thomas succeeds in making readers uncomfortable with the horror films we think we have seen, his insistence on framing texts with conflicting verbal or visual signifiers that betray each other's artifice remains the key to his sense of political responsibility, a compromise between finding facile villains and overlooking cruelty. "Anne weeps for all sentient beings," his blackout narrator reflects. "And I know my brother

Ishmael cusses. I'm too mean for either of that" (115). With all the didactic play in his text-paratext pairings and the exhortations that "we must speak or be like patterns on a wall" (111), the last lines of the poem that precedes "Hat Red" are a reminder not to transform the poet's language into a static prophecy that defers the reader's own response: "You don't have to take my word / For 'it'" (111).

## Johanna Drucker's Paratextual Histories

Where Thomas deconstructs gothic characterizations, Drucker presents her own versions of communal histories in books that mimic the structure of a palimpsest but that challenge the authority of both paratextual source and poetic revision from the onset. Drucker's books also offer a transition from the characteristic divided formats that I have discussed in many of the earlier chapters; instead, she expands the visual collage of a piece like Bernstein's "Artifice of Absorption" to show interactions among multiple sources on the page space.

Drucker is a book artist, a poet, a printer, and an art historian.[6] Her artist's books span a period from the seventies to the present, combining poetic narrative sequences, typographic play, and illustrations or found texts. Many of these print experiments go back to her scholarly interest in typography in the early-twentieth-century avant-garde manifestos and journals. What she strives for in her own essays and creative writing is a theoretical model of materiality that examines the systemic structures of the language and the physicality of its transcription, as well as the ways in which these elements are mediated by historical context and subjective taste (*VW* 43–46).

Like Thomas and Howe, Drucker explores constructions of subjectivity by analyzing "who gets put into and left out of the network text(ure)" of specific cultural narratives (*S* 2). The difference lies, I have observed, with the status of their sources. Both Howe and Thomas require outside research into their paratexts, while Drucker, in her two 1990 artist's books, creates on the page space all material traces of the paratextual documents whose premises she then subverts. What is at stake in inventing these authoritative paratexts and what does it mean to describe a female subject, as she does in *Simulant Portrait,* making "slow progress toward a reinhabitation of an unreal past from which she, normally, would merely and systematically have been excluded" (47)? The description emphasizes the fictiveness of any historian's claim to represent events accurately, but it also suggests that the strategy of reinhabiting a simulation gives the artist the freedom to develop her own forms and political agendas.

Drucker's experimentation with invented source histories in the earlier 1990 book, *The History of the/my Wor(l)d,* produces a quirkily allusive text that reinterprets civilization from Genesis to late capitalism with particular attention to American myths of origin.[7] As the title reference to "the/my Wor(l)d" suggests, the book is divided like a palimpsest on every page into two discrete narratives, in this case with clear typographic distinctions between source and revision. One immediately notices the paratextual "source," modeled on the easily absorbed summaries in an illustrated grade school history primer; it is a record in large black print of "LAW" (*H* 6), founding "father figures" (5), and "conquerors" (15) that she uses to "undermin[e] the meta-narrative of history through its own clichés" (*FW* 308). Despite the parodic distortions, the source does present readily recognizable biblical and historical allusions: Exodus, the Renaissance, colonialism, the Industrial Revolution. Pivotal events involve the settling of frontiers, which, as for Howe, are moments of closure and conventionalization. The New World is opened for settlement in a sentence whose overblown capitals diminish Plymouth Rock to a continental "doormat" in a history of crudely "hacked" expansions, humorously implying that America was colonized for the sake of a ritual Thanksgiving meal (*H* 23) (see fig. 6.6). Stock references to Indians, cowboys,

Fig. 6.6. Excerpt from Johanna Drucker, *The History of the/my Wor(l)d*, p. 23. The portions printed in red in the original are reproduced here in gray. Copyright 1990, 1995 by Johanna Drucker. Reprinted by permission of Granary Books.

and pioneers throughout the book are in fact interspersed with fifties icons of turkey dinners and hamburger plates as if these symbols of homogenized consumption were the inevitable outcome of the first homesteads, an ironic projection that undercuts the promise of an "instant of independence" (23).

The second layer in this mock palimpsest is a small-font narrative in red ink (reproduced in gray in fig. 6.6) that inserts details about domesticity and sexuality. Drucker associates them with the memory of her mother and her own education in a mother tongue (*FW* 308), but the references also describe the education of less articulate subjects throughout different historical periods. The black-ink Thanksgiving passage in figure 6.6 is interrupted by red lines about "children boarded into schools with unforgiving mistresses and strict orderings of the day" (*H* 23), the left-hand diagram of a science specimen suggestively depicting the students as supervised experiments. Another page's "benefactors" and "stable seeming institutions" in black are flanked by red-ink comments about a "dark passage," or perhaps rite of passage, in which a subject learns to assume "a mask of passion" exemplified by a lipsticked smile (31).

The structural similarity to palimpsests by Howe or Waldrop, however, is ultimately misleading. To create a palimpsest from one's own self-parodic source already blurs the distinction between paratext and overwriting, making it difficult to theorize either original crimes or rebellions. Drucker further complicates the text-paratext relation through her annotated illustrations.[8] The numbered figures, often advertising icons, in both black and red narratives satirize the premise of a demonstrably true version of history, no matter which narrator does the retelling. The pictures are accompanied by notes in tiny black print, a run-

Fig. 6.7. Detail from Johanna Drucker, *The History of the/my Wor(l)d*, p. 21. Copyright 1990, 1995 by Johanna Drucker. Reprinted by permission of Granary Books.

36. The alien confronted them with menacing force across the desk; how else could they deal with the contract under such circumstances.

ning commentary on monsters, devils, and invading aliens that defamiliarizes the records of both public and domestic pursuits. Businessmen in black fend off alien negotiators at the conference table—aliens who look exactly like the humans (see fig. 6.7)—only to come home to red-ink goods transformed into equally alienated objects of scrutiny: a refrigerator whose "Frozen assets" are described as an Ice Age "mammoth" (*H* 35) or a suburban lawn mower that gets used for shaving. The illustrations for public or private narratives, moreover, are increasingly difficult to distinguish. Construction sites and community buildings are just as likely to be printed in red ink, while a note about "the sign of the passion—flaming red" is illustrated by an unromantic lobster pointedly printed in black (9).

The lack of distinction between public and private references in these pictures calls our attention to the fact that Drucker's red-print text does not provide alternative narratives of identity for marginalized subject positions nor even a countertradition of named dissenters, as we might find in Howe's essays. Drucker instead heightens the tension between scattering and recovery in the poetic palimpsest form by creating an elaborate textual striptease. The black text reminds us that "the rest of the world whose history is unwritten here and elsewhere developed apace apart" (*H* 26), while the fine red print promises an erotic interiority, a glimpse at "secret notebooks" (21) that are never revealed. The nineteenth-century woman, for instance, remains a literary abstraction, a "heroine densely trapped in plots and vapors" inhabiting "empty houses full of secret passages and spells played out as rituals" (26) without explicit details, one more vignette in the red text's "pocket[s] of repressed behavior" (7) or "traces locked in drawers to which the key had been abandoned" (33). The "witnesses" to "private lives" in Drucker's fine red print always seem "bound and gagged to remain immutably / complicit and anonymous" in their own representations (28); for once, all but the last three words of this small-font description are printed in black as if to underscore the extent of that complicit self-displacement.

The sensual tease of secret notebooks that cannot be fully decoded is part of the beautiful crafting of the book itself as an art object, a slim 10" × 13" volume with black and red letterpress lines flanked by the printed found texts: the diagrams, sketches, and photographs. The reader's consciousness of the artist's materials and labor might create a sense of intimate contact between author and audience, but the narrative always underscores the artifice of that seeming intimacy. When Drucker, along with the name of her publishing imprint, Druckwerk, literally make a cameo appearance on the last page, she enters as an art object, the portrait of a frontier woman on a brooch, rather than a snapshot of the author that might put a personal face on "the/my" world (see fig. 6.8). The cameo Drucker remains in the objective case, "me" (*H* 40), demonstrating the difficulty of trying to situate "one who was her" (27), a woman slipping between subject and object positions and between different historical perspectives ("who was I is I" [27]). In the end, we are not sure if the declaration that the author is taking her "tongue back into [her] lap" (40) is an eroticized retraction or a reclamation of language.

Fig. 6.8. Detail from Johanna Drucker, *The History of the/my Wor(l)d*, p. 40. Copyright 1990, 1995 by Johanna Drucker. Reprinted by permission of Granary Books.

me

DRUCKWERK
&
GRANARY BOOKS

These narrative ambiguities and evasions allow Drucker to move from the text-paratext division of a palimpsest to a series of simultaneous story lines, graphics, and typographic symbols spread on the page space or running across page breaks. An invented paratext breaks the linear relation between source and revision, freeing the narrator to create her own revolutionary predecessors or multiple points of origin, a process that occurs to some degree, Drucker suggests—although more covertly—in any history interpreted as "manifest destiny" (*H* 24). What looks like a record of patriarchs and landmark events in her *History* is exposed as a set of mythic precursors established retroactively with each successive innovation. "[T]ales of pyramids and picture language" exist as rumors circulated through the contemporary mail (13). An American cowboy ushers in the narrative of the European Renaissance, as if asserting America's own cultural claims, while the initial "shining promise" of the "NEW WORLD" (21) is read backward from the picture of a modern worker fingering his dollar bills (20).

The effect of these continually reformulated origins and addresses is to situate the reader in different subject positions as abruptly as the black or red texts move from one character to another. At times, the narrator addresses the audience with a "we" that alternately affirms a consensus against external foes ("the enemy was playing hardball with our hearts and minds" [*H* 31]) and suggests a band of social outcasts ("repartée . . . raked us" [18]). At other times, the reader follows more distanced stories of "her" or "them" struggling "to find a clue to their own identity" (18). The reader may be titillated by the hinted "stuff of dreams" that "thrill[s] the prepubescent limbs with unspeakable urges" in these vignettes (24) but nevertheless remains in the position of the prim young miss at the telephone who eavesdrops on an older girl's conversations as "enemy lines" that she never entirely understands: "one cryptic story after another" (24) (see fig. 6.9). The narrator implies that the reader as eavesdropper, inexperienced and guiltily aroused, with a mixed sense of participation in and exclusion from the overheard exchanges, is a fitting symbol for the fallacies of communal historiography. It is preferable, she argues, to an audience looking for a "border patrol" to "mak[e] sure they were in the right place in their reading" (39), playing a "cops and robbers game of understanding" (38) without regard for "the other forms of innocence consumed" (39) in the process of establishing their preferred version of history.

As the interest in transgressive reading strategies and the echoes of the palimpsest structure suggest, Drucker's book is not simply a parody of conventional history texts. It becomes an oblique commentary on the use of paratexts themselves—on readers' expectations, for example, that artistic experiments will be framed by an explanatory narrative or by traditional source documents. Drucker reexamines both the paratextual formats of *History* and its model for reader participation in *Simulant Portrait,* a book that she composed during the summer of 1990.[9]

Fig. 6.9. Detail from Johanna Drucker, *The History of the/my Wor(l)d,* p. 24. Copyright 1990, 1995 by Johanna Drucker. Reprinted by permission of Granary Books.

44. From behind enemy lines there were mysterious telecommunications; we listened in on the upstairs line while she told one cryptic story after another.

*Simulant Portrait* is presented as a pulp celebrity biography with a twist; purportedly written in 2050, it is the futuristic story of the first "simulant," or artificially engineered person. Despite the *Blade Runner* premise, there are strong formal resemblances between this text and *History*. Both books adapt a loose palimpsest structure of paratextual history and disruptive revision. The biographer's narrative, with its large-print titles and documentary evidence, serves as the source history in *Simulant;* it is intersected by diary entries that emphasize errors and blind spots in the records. As in *History,* moreover, both public narrative and private revision are revealed as equally fictive constructs, since all records of the simulant's identity, including her personal memories, have been fabricated.

What is different from *History* is the approach to the paratext. The simulant herself authorizes the biographer to "invent the narrative" of her life from its documentary traces, to "reify the persona of which these discrete bits were the defining points" (*S* inside dust cover), fully aware that any attempt at narrative order is a false imposition. The book thus becomes an overt interrogation of the relation between experimental texts and readerly paratexts. The central question is why the simulant—a fragmented "composition" that can never be resolved into a coherent whole—wants an explanatory narrative of its own experiment, particularly the aggressively publicized narrative that we get here. Whereas *History* features fifties marketing icons, this 2050 biography goes even further in its popular culture forays, combining convoluted literary sentences with echoes of tabloid exposés, pulp fiction romances, movie scripts, and advertisements; its illustrations include family portraits and digitized printouts of faces. The book, indeed, seems composed entirely of publicity statements without a clear referent, as if paratextual documents had openly become the primary art form. The authorized biography usurps most of the page space with its summaries and evidence; the simulant's diary entries are incorporated within its commentary. Even more graphically than in *History,* the result is an explosion of multiple source presentations that compete with and contradict each other's authority.

The opening chapter about the simulant's origins sets the book's tone with announcements that emphasize their own misdirections. As a record of the simulant's "HUMBLE BEGINNINGS" in chapter 1, the inscription "SAVING FACE" (*S* 6) contrasts ironically with the averted gaze or censored eyes of the women in the photographs (see fig. 6.10). The large face in the main shot, presumably the adult simulant's, lies half in shadow, while the white blanket draped over the mother's dress in the oval inset takes up a third of the frame like a metaphorical erasure of the foreground. The biographer's remark that Sim-one was "Born normal" (8) is prefaced by the headline reminder that she was "NOT BORN" at all (see fig. 6.11), and dates are replaced by conflicting abstractions: "Too soon: high time" (7). The "evidence" of her origins suggested in the boxed abstractions, the note reveals, is "Mythic" only in the sense of being illusory (7). Linking the search for "Familiar struggles" and "primary emotions" to "the hearts of readers who had long since vanished" (7) only offers the simulant's biography as a mock-nostalgic re-creation of sentimental narrative.

The humorous anxiety over sexual and textual reproduction in these fake origins suggests broader questions about the use of paratexts to determine the

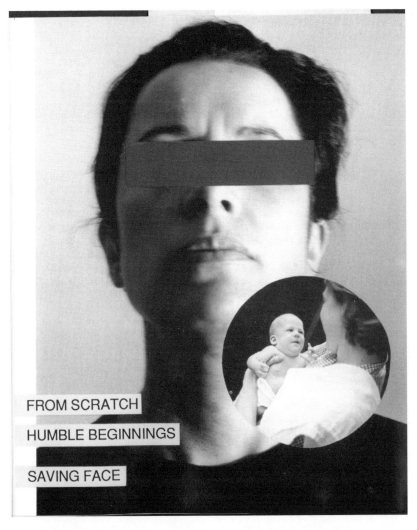

Fig. 6.10. Excerpt from Johanna Drucker, *Simulant Portrait*, p. 6. Copyright 1990 by Johanna Drucker. Reprinted by permission of Pyramid Atlantic and Johanna Drucker.

public reception and transmission of a "prototype" artistic text (7). Do poets' essays and source references, no matter how creative, play to readers' desire for an authoritative interpretation, an inside scoop, a fiction of authorial presence, or a familiar analogy to help categorize an indeterminate text? By deconstructing a paratext into highlighted references, digressive notes, and mutually exclusive supporting details, Drucker goes further than either Spicer or Bernstein in frustrating the possibility of conventional exegesis while at the same time she still

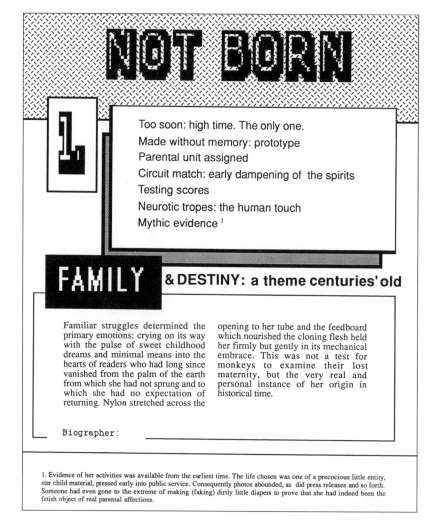

Fig. 6.11. Excerpt from Johanna Drucker, *Simulant Portrait*, p. 7. Copyright 1990 by Johanna Drucker. Reprinted by permission of Pyramid Atlantic and Johanna Drucker.

uses a language of soap opera scandals and Victorian romances to entice us into closer reading: "Through clouds of thick steam her heart poured onto the pavements and where was He, the hero of our story, at the time?" (*S* 32). The sentences collapse into amorphously suggestive references and unfinished confessions.

There is only one clearly identified relationship in the text that does provide the intimate, erotic, (re)productive details that were deferred in *History:* it is the collaboration itself between the simulant and the biographer reading the significance of her archives. "[S]he, while I watched," the biographer coyly writes, "bent down in modest adoration of the thing wrought which was hers, in essence, though surrogate in inception. I was happy to place it in her hands, this figment of our wild imaginings, and watch the slow turning of its faceted reflection in her eyes" (*S* 5). In contrast to the inexperienced eavesdropper in *History,* it is the reader as creative artist that fascinates Drucker here, a ghostwriter who can reassemble an experimental text through his or her own imaginative reflections.

The biographer herself describes this "surrogate" creation with the simulant as very close to a manifesto form:

> She loved the big, sloppy, melodramatic text I wrote for her—that slushy, pulpy prose which vibrated on the page like bad copy from the retrospective exhibition of a mediocre artist, or blurbs on the jacket of an unknown recording artist, bluffing its claims in overblown language. She had, herself, chosen the files of artist types from which to make her self, her soul, her story, having decided they got the best prose treatment in the anecdotal versions of their lives. (*S* 5)

The flamboyant publicity notes emphasizing a dual sense of inflated artistic importance and radical marginality recall the rhetoric of the early-twentieth-century avant-garde manifestos. *Simulant Portrait* does reflect the manifesto styles that Drucker admires—what she describes as Marinetti's "cybernetic" imagination (*VW* 109) or Tzara's adaptations of advertising formats. Yet the difference between a manifesto and this description of the biography is also instructive. Drucker's contemporary simulant does not wish to write her own paratext; she wants exhibition notes written by someone else so that she can step into a ready-made revolutionary tradition that exists as a shared fiction with at least one other participant.

Why does Drucker insist on this imaginary collaboration between the simulant and an external reader? The fact that the reading/ghostwriting takes place against background references to a "public bid for independence" (*S* 25), a "SOCIAL CONTRACT" (19), or "CONTRACTS" that "Dematerialise with Public Whim" (20) evokes the assumption of a consenting audience in American revolutionary political documents. One could argue that Drucker simply plays here with the fiction of an ideal reader, a close reflection of "the/my self" (2) who, like Howe's reader-reviser, will be able to continue the poet's process. Drucker symbolically creates the biographer in her image by signing the preface with her own scribbled name.

Yet the interest in outside commentary and the retrospective glance at early manifestos raise questions posed by the other postwar poets in this study. What new forms replace the stereotype of the manifesto artist-hero making claims for a vision of nationalism or consensus? To whom or for whom does the contemporary avant-gardist speak? "Worn thin on the hard edges" of a "modernist mode," the simulant cannot tell if her own audience is real or fictional: "she gave a public speech to a fictional audience which over time became real as any other bar scene where everyone took turns in the same melodramatic sequence" (*S* 21). Drucker may be satirizing the avant-gardists' claims of an interested audience, or she may be implying that manifesto rhetoric has become so familiar that anyone can mimic its theatrics, if not the substance of its agendas.

But *Simulant Portrait* also answers charges about the co-optation of an avant-garde art with the idea that the more familiar the paratextual formulas become, the more readily the artist can go beyond readers' expectations of those traditions. The multiplied worker-machines in Marinetti's manifestos come to life as a female simulant who dictates her own presentation. Authorizing histories break down under the weight of their own contradictory documentation as the book rewrites the structure of the palimpsest genre. There are no guarantees made, moreover, about the reception of these changes. *Simulant Portrait*'s romance with the close reader exists side by side with the conviction that a sympathetic reflection on the artist's message and style is what one is least likely to get from critics. For every reader who admits her own uncertainty about interpretations, there are boxes of letters to the simulant full of polite platitudes or dismissals. The one query, "How have you been?" pasted on the simulant's mirror (47) opens a postcard so trite that other archivists refuse to take it—hardly exhibition material. Drucker's point in mentioning these notes in the biographer's narrative seems to be that even the silence, resistance, or misinterpretations of less sympathetic readers must be factored into the process of an avant-garde composition if it is to expand its experimental parameters.

The early-twentieth-century Futurists and Dadaists often warned readers not to trust any histories written about their movements. Drucker's book challenges readers to write their own account of contemporary avant-garde texts but to write it with the knowledge that it cannot provide a satisfactory explanation to make all the fragments cohere and that it will probably turn out to be a different kind of participatory creativity than the authors had envisioned. Her paratexts open up the possibility that is already implicit, despite the different formats, in Olson's parenthetical qualifications, in Spicer's letters and translations, in Howe's series of marginalia, and in Bernstein's mixed text-paratexts that always seem to respond to the latest critical commentary on his previous book: the reader's response, however unpredictable, adds at least one more intertext to the poetry for the next revisionary construction of a public space. Drucker's biographer, continually searching for a new rumor or interpretive report to insert in the simulant's narrative, admits that such readerly intrusions may be the "most flimsy map of the territory" the artist is "destined to occupy" (*S* 47). But the very insufficiency of the descriptive map after "All the documents have been exhibited" (39) also indicates that there may still be some vestige of frontier left open for the avant-gardist to explore.

Notes

·

Works Cited and Consulted

·

Index

# Notes

### 1. Introduction

1. "Getting Ready To Have Been Frightened" was published in *Roof* 8 in 1978 and reprinted, with minor changes, as the title poem in *Getting Ready To Have Been Frightened* (1988); the quote and page layout are reproduced from the book version.

2. My use of the term thus differs from its more general definition in Gérard Genette's two comprehensive studies translated as *Palimpsests* and *Paratexts*. He describes the paratext as any inscription that presents the text to a specific public, including such forms as the preface, cover, title, table of contents, and publisher's notes, tracing each device across multiple national literatures and centuries. My focus on creative authorial notes, essays, and source documents that no longer occupy a secondary status to the text is integral to the study of an avant-garde poetic tradition, both in the turn-of-the-century manifesto forms and in the contemporary text-paratext pairings.

3. I begin with the early-twentieth-century Futurist manifestos because of the extensive experimentation with the genre as a literary form and the parallels with contemporary avant-garde rhetoric. Although there are thematic echoes in recent American paratexts of Romantic debates over the public role of poetry, Wordsworth's preface to the second *Lyrical Ballads* and Shelley's "A Defence of Poetry," for instance, still keep more of the conventions of the critical essay with clearly structured paragraphs of arguments and examples. Even if one reads the Futurists' diatribes against Romanticism, moreover, as the struggle with a preceding movement, the Futurists' emphasis both on agonistic de-creation and on shaping specific political agendas tends to be even more pronounced than in the British Romantic rhetoric of poet-legislators. The celebration of technological production also contrasts with the early Romantic idealization of nature.

4. The manifesto artists' alternating descriptions of their contact with a public and their status as an isolated vanguard prophesying a future state, as well as their stylistic challenge to familiar modes of reading even while using forums like newspapers or leaflets, set them apart from Benedict Anderson's imagined communities, for example, in which language users' sense of simultaneous partici-

pation in a nation is reflected in the experience of reading popular genres such as the novel and the newspaper or is inculcated by a state education system.

5. For a study specifically of the significance of typographic experimentation as part of the manifestos' politics, see too Johanna Drucker, *The Visible Word.*

6. As the previously cited manifesto excerpts indicate, this language of destroying the past is a defining component of early-twentieth-century Continental avant-garde rhetoric, though there are variations on which traditions—usually the immediate precursors—are to be rejected. The Russian neoprimitivists, for instance, rejected more contemporary naturalistic styles of painting or salon art while valorizing an older heritage symbolized by folk art. The idealization of a primitive past differs from what I describe as an American avant-garde preoccupation with ambiguous origins and ongoing textual attempts to formulate a national identity.

7. Fredman not only traces the continuing influence of Emerson's themes but also analyzes the generative sentences in Emerson's prose as an early model for twentieth-century prose-poetic texts like Williams's *Kora in Hell.* While his study *Poet's Prose* concentrates on creative forms that reflect a stance of "receptivity" and "accommodation" rather than the egoistic impositions that he associates with verse epics (8), the American paratexts that I discuss, particularly the ones before World War II, do not necessarily fit that stance.

8. Among recent texts, John Lowney also discusses Williams's idea of descent as a "quest for origins or 'ground' that presupposes an initial dislocation or displacement" (26), going back to Joseph Riddel's argument in *The Inverted Bell* that Williams reads American poetry as a project in search of its own authorizing myths, a search that is always-already mediated by interpretation. Lowney does not focus on paratexts but defines Williams's avant-gardism in more general terms of poetic experimentation with multiple social discourses toward the goal of uniting art and praxis (17).

9. See too Bob Perelman's argument in *The Trouble with Genius* that Pound's literary and political statements cannot easily be separated, since Pound's writing as a whole expresses the inherent contradictions in modernist texts that claim the social importance of aesthetically difficult styles (31) or that associate a public with commodified mass culture and yet court public attention with extraliterary forms (4–5).

10. Richard Kostelanetz, for example, who is unimpressed by contemporary Language experiments, makes this point succinctly in his entry on Charles Bernstein in the *Dictionary of the Avant-Gardes,* linking Bernstein's essays to Marinetti's publicizing manifestos and arguing that Language poetic theories are more interesting than the poems (21).

11. Steven Clay and Rodney Phillips offer an extended history of these and other journals of the mimeograph revolution.

12. See Joseph Conte's analysis of the Black Mountain poets' formal adaptations of field models or von Hallberg's discussion in *American Poetry and Culture* of systems in the imagery and composition techniques of Olson, Creeley, and Ashbery.

13. Bernstein has commented that Mac Low's chance-determined writing through Pound's poem undermines the formal and political "authoritarianism" in *The Cantos*, noting particularly the absence of voice symbolized by the concluding blank page in Mac Low's text (*MW* 165).

14. The translations of an earlier poet like Pound, as Lawrence Venuti points out, also challenge the transparency of the signified and foreground the foreignness of the source. The opacity of the Zukofskys' *Catullus*, however, is far more pronounced than in Pound's translations, and Spicer's *After Lorca* also explicitly theorizes the implications of its own distortions and inventions.

## 2. Parentheses and Presentation Prose: Community in Charles Olson's Paratexts

1. Olson explains in *The Special View of History* that Herodotus's "'istorin'" meant "'finding out for oneself,' instead of depending on hearsay" (20). Olson's *'istorin* is linked to the polis as "localism" (25), but also to Jane Harrison's sense of myth as something "'popular,' i.e. collective" (23).

2. In 1952, after being awakened and questioned by Bureau agents, Olson wrote to Robert Creeley that the agents had turned "HISTORY"—his personal history and associations, as well as the *'istorin* of a free polis—into "a LIE right there in front of me in my own parlor" (*Charles Olson and Robert Creeley* 70).

3. This approach is best exemplified by Robert von Hallberg's seminal study of Olson as poet-pedagogue, *Charles Olson: The Scholar's Art*. He explains Olson's syntactic experimentation in the complex early poetry either as the poet's response to a world of flux in which any description must be continually reformulated (72) or as a technique that emphasizes the poet's "forceful tone, self-confident enough to take the time to say everything that ought to be said, even if infinitives must be split by inserted parenthetical phrases" (38) and an initial address must be recontextualized. Subsequent critical texts, such as Don Byrd's extensive study of *The Maximus Poems* as a whole, have placed greater emphasis on the importance of Olson's disjunctions and "rough edges" in the poetic pedagogy (112), though they do not discuss the specific implications of Olson's blurred distinction between text and parenthetical paratext that I suggest here.

4. Both von Hallberg (*Charles Olson*) and David Kellogg note that the open

parenthesis symbolizes a new type of history; I address the stylistic feature itself as a key component of Olson's postwar poetry.

5. I am indebted for the reference to George F. Butterick's note on the line in *A Guide to* The Maximus Poems *of Charles Olson* (17).

6. Olson gratefully acknowledged this assistance by dedicating the prose-poetic essay "Proprioception" to Jones.

7. Continuing the argument he began in *Poet's Prose,* Fredman asserts in *The Grounding of American Poetry* that American vanguard poets, confronted with a sense of cultural groundlessness, use prose statements of poetics to create an interpretive context for their experiments. He analyzes Olson's essays and lectures as examples of documents that "authoriz[e]" a writer's poems (3) rather than as creative prose poems in themselves, although that distinction, I have suggested, is difficult to uphold in Olson's paratexts.

Though his discussion primarily concerns poets' appropriations of the natural, see too Philip Kuberski's placement of prose pieces like "Projective Verse" and *Mayan Letters* in an American cultural tradition of asserting the authority of an innovative claim by linking it to an older discourse (175), a gesture that reflects the "American concern with the artificiality, the historic nature of its myths" (192).

8. Tom Clark points out that Olson had felt the letters were significant enough to retain carbons and argues that he saw his letters generally as a creative forum for exploring subject material that he wished to incorporate into his poetry (197).

9. Olson's interpretation of the glyphs and of a human universe has been the subject of extensive critical interrogation. Thomas Bertonneau reads Olson's Mayan communal glyphs as part of the conflict in a postmodernist poetics that still insists on a discoverable referent for the "human" (120). He critiques Olson's approach for overlooking the role of sacrificial violence in culture-making in the Mayan myths. Fredman, who notes Olson's fascination with the Maya's self-grounding in their own bodies as a simultaneous gesture of communal openness (*Grounding* 43), suggests that Olson uses the symbol of the glyph in his "Causal Mythology" vision of the Maximus-poet as an image of the "human possibility" of expression, a possibility that "one both participates in and represents" (89). Yet I would also emphasize the degree to which the persona in *Mayan Letters* problematizes his own mythic image, betraying an uncertainty over communicating his glyphic interpretations even in the correspondence to a close member of his own poetic community. In terms of stylistic analysis of the *Mayan Letters,* Kuberski has pointed out their interruptions and abstractions. Olson's Mayan glyphs, he asserts, are a "natural" language that can never be fully theorized, the fetishized origin-Other of Olson's own "artificial" (185) prose statements that affect a macho "roughness" (191) only to reemphasize the loss of those natural

signs. Olson, I argue, is more self-conscious of the limitations and breaks in his cultural translation project, particularly in context of his audience address in *Mayan Letters.*

10. Olson mentions Sauer's "Environment and Culture During the Last De-glaciation" in both "A Bibliography on America for Ed Dorn" and *Pleistocene Man. Pleistocene Man* also alludes to Sauer's *Man in Nature: America Before the Days of the White Men* and "Time and Place in Ancient America" published in *Landscape* 6.2.

11. See too George Hutchinson's contention that Olson's interest in Paleolithic spoken language and in cave art is tied to his belief in poetic language as a tool for collective education, specifically the communication of a projective stance that might be able to reform the contemporary polis as well. He interprets Olson's fascination with Mayan glyphs as a direct extension of his interest in Pleistocene culture rather than a different approach to the reader's role.

12. Charles Doria, for example, argues that Olson uses metaphors of grade school instruction in this essay because the Pleistocene "is supposed to attack, modify, and re-train the poetic sensibility" on "a very primary level" (138). Yet the argument leads to a certain defensiveness about Olson's style; Doria comments that the writing disrupts familiar thought processes at the same that he insists the text is not as "nebulous" as it seems (137).

13. Susan Howe, for whom Olson has been an important stylistic influence, acknowledges these typecast roles of women in his poetry while valorizing the "feminine" aspect of his poetics in *The Birth-mark* (180–81) and "Where Should the Commander Be." See too Robert O'Brien Hokanson's analysis of the gen-der ideologies behind both Olson's female archetypes and his poetic praxis.

## 3. "Created to Explain": Jack Spicer's Exegetical Paratexts

1. Blaser tentatively gives the letter's date as 1957, when Spicer had returned to California from the East Coast ("Letters" 46–47).

2. In addition to Spicer's reluctance to use nonlocal publishers, his post-1956 serial poems, in which the book rather than the individual lyric is the unit, have also presented difficulties for anthologists. Donald Allen included four of the "Imaginary Elegies" from Spicer's early poetry in *The New American Poetry: 1945–1960.* The Norton anthology *Postmodern American Poetry* (1994) and *American Poetry Since 1950: Innovators and Outsiders* (1993) are among the more recent collections that include Spicer's writing. Edward Foster in his monograph on Spicer speculates nonetheless, "Thousands of poems and books were written under his tutelage and criticism" (45). There have been special Spicer issues of journals such as *Caterpillar* (1970), *Boundary 2* (1977), *Ironwood* (1986), and *Acts* (1987); an edited volume of Spicer's lectures, *The House That Jack Built* (Gizzi

1998); and a comprehensive Spicer biography, *Poet Be Like God* (Ellingham and Killian 1998), that provides detailed background on the influences and allegiances within Spicer's poetry circle.

3. Spicer lists the American and international authors to whom he sent copies in a letter to Blaser with the approximate date of 1958 ("Letters" 52).

4. Spicer's first Vancouver lecture, "Dictation and 'A Textbook of Poetry,'" explains his model of the poet bombarded with messages from an "Outside" (*L* 5). While his favorite metaphors for that Outside are Martians and ghostly poetic predecessors, the image of the poet as a radio receiving transmissions also suggests more familiar types of cultural broadcasts. Critics have proposed various interpretations of Spicer's Outside in his dialogic or oppositional sense of community; see Blaser, Hatlen, Damon, Foster. Michael Davidson's chapter on Spicer's *kreis* in *The San Francisco Renaissance* focuses not only on Spicer's dialogues with predecessors but also on the daily bar talk and correspondence among *kreis* members. Davidson emphasizes Spicer's need for debate even within that community of sympathetic listeners and sees a Bakhtinian dialogism as the structuring principle of Spicer's post-1956 texts, from the conversational letters inserted in *After Lorca* or the mixed text and commentary of "Homage to Creeley" to the shifts in subject position of *Language* (*San Francisco* 157). Peter Gizzi, who also looks at some of Spicer's divided texts in his afterword to *The House That Jack Built,* stresses Spicer's incorporation of communal discourses beyond the *kreis*—the pop culture references from sports, science fiction, and radio programs, as well as a national political language of invading aliens and paranoia (190).

5. Blaser confirms that Spicer and he were reading Motherwell's anthology *The Dada Painters and Poets* "page by page" in 1956 when the "Unvert Manifesto" was composed (*CB* 351).

6. From Tzara's "Seven Dada Manifestoes":

> A few days ago I attended a gathering of imbeciles. There were lots of people. Everybody was charming. Tristan Tzara, a small, idiotic and insignificant individual, delivered a lecture on the art of becoming charming. And incidentally, he was charming. And witty. Isn't that delicious? (97)

"Charming" occurs particularly frequently in this Motherwell version since the translator, Ralph Manheim, often uses the word for both "charmant" and "sympathique."

7. Maria Damon, one of the few critics who has looked at "The Unvert Manifesto," analyzes the poet's ambivalence toward camp as the signifier of a gay community (163–65). Instead of examining camp language either as clowning or as

a vatic openness to difference and transgression, I focus on the way that Dada nonsense games offer the narrator a mediated form of public exposure.

Though he does not discuss "The Unvert Manifesto" specifically, Gizzi mentions Spicer's narrators' erotic courtship of the reader, an "amorous playing for keeps" that also warns away the less serious interpreter (175). He notes a shifting audience address in several of Spicer's texts in which the reader is sometimes privy to the poet's jokes, at other times excluded from them (174).

8. In her analysis of *After Lorca* in "Ghostwriting the Text," Lori Chamberlain describes Spicer's parodic and self-parodic translations of Lorca's love poems as a specifically gay poetic praxis (436); she cites Bruce Boone's analysis of a "'trivializing" stance in gay language that both invites and deflects "connection" because it recognizes the dangers in that contact ("Gay Language" 81, 82).

Clayton Eshleman lays the groundwork for these discussions by pointing out some of Spicer's particularly awkward translations, though his interpretations are hampered by his distinction between arbitrary versus deliberate translation choices. In the latter category, he speculates that Spicer may have chosen "big" in "The Ballad of Weeping" to approximate spoken language rather than literary diction (37).

9. Critics have tended to take Spicer at his word when he describes his poetry as dictation and cites *The Heads of the Town Up to the Aether,* or particularly "A Textbook of Poetry," as a composition "as near to dictation, without interference from me, as I've written" (*L* 19). Norman Finkelstein puts the case most strongly when he states that Spicer in *The Heads of the Town* "renounces all sense of poetic personality and empties himself completely, so that the ghostly voices of language may speak" (90), demonstrating a poetics that is "the furthest possible extension of Keats's Negative Capability" (99).

10. See too Boone's comments in "Spicer's Writing" on Spicer's infernal cityscapes as a nightmare version of Olson's polis in ruins where marginalized subjects submit to those who oppress them.

11. Both Davidson and John Granger analyze Spicer's play with the exegetical limits of human language. In Spicer's theology, Davidson argues, no language suffices to describe God, and the poet therefore relies on punning word play that foregrounds its own semantic slippages and metaphoric substitutions to reflect the inexplicable incarnation of the Logos as Lowghost (*San Francisco* 162). Granger also speaks of Spicer's negative theology with narrators who are "blinded by a 'sudden illumination,' an astonishment at the limit of their own horizon" (167), and who vacillate between hermeneutical investigation and the "fictive play" of language (176). He focuses less on specific issues of audience in "A Textbook of Poetry" or in the structural divisions between poetry and paratextual exegesis per se.

## 4. The Palimpsest as Communal Lyric: Susan Howe's Paratextual Sources

1. Speaking from their own poetic interests and their analyses of other experimental women writers, both Rachel Blau DuPlessis and Kathleen Fraser discuss H.D.'s metaphor of palimpsest in which earlier traces of the female/maternal are imperfectly erased. In DuPlessis's modified Kristevan reading, the palimpsest is a "visual image of the situation of writing" in which the marks and rhythms of the chora are overwritten by the symbolic order and yet those marks can now be read as signs themselves (86). Fraser sees H.D.'s palimpsest as the recovered text of female myths as well as signs "from one's own unconscious" or "a female collective consciousness" that have been overlooked by the "dominant culture" (155). Cynthia Hogue, responding to these two essays, looks at palimpsest in the poetry of Fraser and Howe as a strategy for deconstructing patriarchal images in favor of new feminist models of performative subjectivity.

Ming-Qian Ma in "Articulating the Inarticulate" specifically analyzes the tripartite structure of Howe's palimpsests as she writes through a source to reveal the contradictions within its language that gesture toward a countermethod of active, transgressive knowing rather than static knowledge.

2. Howe explains her interest in René Thom's definition of singularity in her Foster interview in *The Birth-mark* (173). Among discussions of medial noise in Howe's poetic palimpsests, see too Craig Dworkin.

3. Marjorie Perloff in *Poetic License* analyzes the intersection of historical narrative and lyric in Howe's texts, examining Howe's construction of subjects through the juxtaposition of multiple styles and documentary fragments. Lynn Keller scrutinizes Howe's fascination with recovering individual voices at the same time that these subjects are accessible only through elliptical archival and literary traces or explicitly foregrounded as the poet's own slanted interpretation (194). Linda Reinfeld argues that Howe's "capacity for appropriation is at least as great as her capacity to identify with those who suffer as a consequence of having been unfairly appropriated" (136) as the authorial self "merges and collides with its object" of study (137). Howe's idea of voice, Peter Nicholls suggests, is an artful collage of different sources (589), while Nicky Marsh interrogates Howe's seemingly conflicting creations of self-absenting narrators along with an autobiographical "I" voice (126).

4. Howe's rhetoric of the feminization of antinomian dissent has been well noted; see Keller, DuPlessis.

5. See too Ma's detailed reading of Howe's visually disjunctive layout and word play in "Scattering As Behavior Toward Risk" as a challenge to the linguistic structure of a patriarchal history ("Poetry as History Revised").

6. Perloff concurs with Don Byrd and Michael Palmer in placing *My Emily Dickinson,* for instance, in the tradition of Olson's *Call Me Ishmael* or Duncan's *The H.D. Book,* "texts in which one poet meditates so intensely on the work of another that the two voices imperceptibly merge" (*Poetic License* 36).

7. For an extended discussion of the thematic role of forgery in "A Bibliography," see W. Scott Howard.

8. Megan Williams observes the conflict in Howe's writing between a desire to preserve her texts for posterity and her mistrust of canons, focusing on excerpts from Howe's interviews to frame a reading of "Melville's Marginalia," although there are suggestive closing remarks about *The Birth-mark.* I argue that the need for a witnessing community is foregrounded in the essays as a response to the scattering of the sources in the poetic palimpsests.

9. John Palattella also notes Howe's tendency to read antinomian enthusiasts both as part of a Puritan iconoclast tradition and as figures marginalized by the Puritans' own civil authority (79).

10. In reading Howe through Michel Serres, Gregory Dale Adamson looks at Howe's depiction of Hutchinson as a communal scapegoat, the Pythagorean irrational that must be excluded to establish social order, though he characterizes *The Birth-mark*'s format more in terms of chaotic noise as a continuation of the poetic palimpsests than a shift away from the scattering approach.

11. In his chapter on "palimtexts," the material traces of writing as an ongoing compositional process, Michael Davidson discusses Howe's interest in writing through manuscript pages as a "salvage historicism" (*Ghostlier Demarcations* 78) that uses textual archives to retrieve both poetic experimentation and signifiers of cultural marginalization.

## 5. "The Constitution of Public Space": Charles Bernstein's Language Paratexts

1. While I focus upon $L=A=N=G=U=A=G=E$ for the Bernstein discussion, for broader coverage of other Language-centered journals, see the selections in Clay and Phillips or my survey essay on little magazines and early Language poetry.

2. Debates over the definition and the value of Language poetry tend to reflect the poets' descriptions of themselves as part of an avant-garde tradition. George Hartley links authors such as Bernstein, Silliman, Andrews, Hejinian, and Perelman to turn-of-the-century European avant-gardes because of their stance against mainstream aesthetic practices, their interest in ideology, and their experiments with grammar and typography. Perloff in *The Dance of the Intellect* places the Language authors in a Poundian avant-garde tradition for their experi-

ments with syntax and their textual integrations of prose and poetry, as well as of poetry and theory. Lazer associates Language writing with "oppositional" early writers such as Williams, Stein, and Zukofsky, with the added influence of poststructuralist criticism. Walter Kalaidjian heralds Language as a postmodern avant-garde because of its commitment to developing new forms of poetic politics and "a genuinely alternative *network* of literary exchange" (323), while Vernon Shetley examines the Language writers' self-conscious production of manifestos. (For some of the early debates over the political ideology of Language writing, see too Charles Altieri, Jed Rasula, and Jerome McGann.) In his descriptions of Language as part of an American avant-garde, Michael Greer points out the problem in trying to summarize a shared political manifesto agenda for highly diverse essays that interrogate the ideology of any definition of poetry. The conflict within the writing between theorizing a poetic or political agenda and negating totalizing statements, I would argue, may be one of Language texts' most characteristically avant-garde features.

3. As Susan Schultz observes, "Language poets like Bernstein know what they want from their readers, and their criticism sets these readers up to make the 'correct' response to the poems" (163). Steve McCaffery argues that the theorization of an indeterminate text to be produced rather than consumed by the reader is itself a highly constructed model of reading. The reader posited in Language theory, Alan Golding qualifies, is a construct shaped specifically in the context of the academy, an audience that can appreciate the critique Language offers of and within those academic institutions (156).

4. Tenney Nathanson has also remarked on the broad utopian rhetoric that recurs in several of Bernstein's essays that suggest experimental poetic language not only as an ideological critique but as an expressive or originary presence, a temporary reversal of alienation (316).

5. Linda Reinfeld analyzes the semantic slippages and the revisions of canonical texts in Bernstein's early poetry, while stressing his interest in the materiality of signifiers as "a new American poetics of presence" against Derridean deconstruction (57).

6. As Paul Naylor notes, individual resistance to characterization is still possible in Bernstein's texts because he derives his linguistic *socious* from Wittgenstein rather than Derrida, situating presence in the use of everyday language; by becoming aware of the language games used to characterize them, the readers can learn to challenge such stereotypes.

7. For this discussion of *A Poetics,* see "Write the Power" in Perelman's *The Marginalization of Poetry.*

8. When questioned further about dialect poetry at a University of Pittsburgh discussion forum, Bernstein drew upon Basil Bernstein's distinction between

speakers limited to one dialect and those with access to multiple dialects, arguing that once exposed to other modes of expression, it is impossible to go back to a "'restricted'" code ("On Poetry" 47).

## 6. Illustrated Histories: The Paratextual Narratives of Lorenzo Thomas and Johanna Drucker

1. Among the few exceptions, see Tom Dent's overview of Thomas's work and Aldon Nielsen's close readings of selected poems.

Thomas has published three poetry collections, a number of small press chapbooks, and his own scholarly studies of African American experimental poetry, most recently *Extraordinary Measures: Afrocentric Modernism and Twentieth-Century American Poetry* (2000). His writing tends to be featured in avant-garde texts such as The Norton *Postmodern American Poetry* and *From the Other Side of the Century* and in African American poetry anthologies that include Umbra writers (e.g., *The Poetry of Black America: Anthology of the Twentieth Century* [1973] and *The Garden Thrives: Twentieth-Century African American Poetry* [1996]).

2. *The Bathers* and *Chances are Few* are Thomas's earliest major collections. Although *Chances are Few* (1979) is advertised on its dust jacket as his "first comprehensive book," the poems in *The Bathers* (1981), which spans his writing of the sixties and seventies, often predate those in *Chances*. Because of these chronological overlaps and the continuity of the gothic themes, I have juxtaposed poems from the two volumes in my discussion.

In terms of the books' visual inserts, Thomas selects the movie stills and reproduced paintings that appear in *Chances are Few*, and he collaborates frequently with his brother, Cecilio Thomas, who designed the collages for *The Bathers*, as well as with other artists.

3. See too Nielsen's analysis of the shifts in speech patterns within a poem such as "Inauguration" as Thomas's way of deconstructing the premise of a monologic American English or a poetic canon.

4. Thomas's poem emphasizes different film incarnations of the Dracula story, and Britton Wilkie's illustrations, which Thomas described as "absolutely *perfect*" (Letter to author, December 7, 1995), draw on images as far back as *Nosferatu*, Murnau's 1922 silent film.

5. During Thomas's 1981 *Callaloo* interview, he commented that the functional idea of the poem "as rhetoric that was to be acted upon" rather than a text "creating consciousness, which will then inspire people to act," was an intermediate "practice" stage that characterized certain black protest writing of the sixties ("'Between the Comedy'" 25).

6. In addition to her artist's books and poetic prose texts such as *Italy*, Drucker's numerous scholarly texts include a seminal monograph of twentieth-century

artists' books, a history of lettering and letter typography, and edited antholo-
gies on visual poetics and multi-media poetry, as well the study of avant-garde
typography in *The Visible Word.*

In terms of reception, Drucker's own artist's books have been discussed by a
few avant-garde poetry critics such as Davidson, Perloff, and Bernstein or have
been analyzed in studies of artists' books like Renée Riese Hubert and Judd D.
Hubert's *The Cutting Edge of Reading: Artists' Books* (1999). Since Drucker's own
scholarship has been prominent in the field of artists' books, she herself provides
commentary on the innovations of her texts in *The Century of Artists' Books* and
*Figuring the Word.*

7. Seventy copies were printed of the original limited 1990 letterpress edi-
tion of *The History of the/my Wor(l)d* at Harvard University's Bow and Arrow Press;
the book was printed offset in 1995 by Granary Books, with the dust jackets done
in letterpress. Although the text is unpaginated, for reference purposes I have
provided page citations beginning with the copyright page as 1.

8. In her reading of *The History of the/my Wor(l)d* ("Johanna Drucker's
Herstory"), Perloff points out that the red and the black texts seem to exchange
positions at the end of this simulated history book, a shift demonstrated in their
illustrations; these reversals and confusions of the two narratives, I argue, take
place all throughout the book's explanatory figures.

9. Drucker designed and produced *Simulant Portrait* during May and June
1990, with three hundred and fifty copies printed offset. This text is also un-
paginated; I number page references beginning with the copyright page as 1.

# Works Cited and Consulted

Adamson, Gregory Dale. "Serres Translates Howe." *SubStance: A Review of Theory and Literary Criticism* 83 (1997): 110–24.

Altieri, Charles. "Without Consequences Is No Politics: A Response to Jerome McGann." von Hallberg, *Politics* 301–7.

Andrews, Bruce. *Getting Ready To Have Been Frightened.* New York: Roof, 1988.

———. "Text and Context." Andrews and Bernstein 31–38.

Andrews, Bruce, and Charles Bernstein, eds. *The L=A=N=G=U=A=G=E Book.* Carbondale: Southern Illinois UP, 1984.

Arteaga, Alfred. *Cantos.* San Jose: Chusma, 1991.

Ashbery, John. *Self-Portrait in a Convex Mirror.* 1975. New York: Penguin, 1976.

Ball, Hugo. "Dada Fragments." Trans. Eugene Jolas. Motherwell 51–54.

Baraka, Amiri. "State/meant." *The LeRoi Jones/Amiri Baraka Reader.* 1960. Ed. William J. Harris. New York: Thunder's Mouth, 1991. 169–70.

Barg, Barbara. "20 Questions." Andrews and Bernstein 136–38.

Benjamin, Walter. "The Work of Art in the Age of Mechanical Reproduction." *Illuminations.* Ed. Hannah Arendt. Trans. Harry Zohn. New York: Schocken, 1969. 217–51.

Bernstein, Charles. *Content's Dream: Essays 1975–1984.* Los Angeles: Sun & Moon, 1986.

———. *Controlling Interests.* New York: Roof, 1980.

———. *Dark City.* Los Angeles: Sun & Moon, 1994.

———. *Islets/Irritations.* 1983. New York: Roof, 1992.

———. *My Way: Speeches and Poems.* Chicago: U of Chicago P, 1999.

———. "On Poetry, Language, and Teaching: A Conversation with Charles Bernstein." *Boundary 2* 23.3 (1996): 45–66.

———. *A Poetics.* Cambridge: Harvard UP, 1992.

———. *Republics of Reality: 1975–1995.* Los Angeles: Sun & Moon, 2000.

———. *Rough Trades.* Los Angeles: Sun & Moon, 1991.

———. *The Sophist.* Los Angeles: Sun & Moon, 1987.

Bertonneau, Thomas. "Life in a Human Universe: Charles Olson's (Post)Modernism in Context (An Anthropoetics)." *Sagetrieb* 13.3 (1994): 117–52.

Blaser, Robin. "The Practice of Outside." *The Collected Books of Jack Spicer.* Ed. Blaser. Santa Rosa: Black Sparrow, 1975. 271–329.

Boone, Bruce. "Gay Language as Political Praxis: The Poetry of Frank O'Hara." *Social Text* 1.1 (1979): 59–92.

———. "Spicer's Writing in Context." *Ironwood* 28 (1986): 202–5.

Bowlt, John E., ed. and trans. *Russian Art of the Avant-Garde: Theory and Criticism 1902–1934.* New York: Viking, 1976. New York: Thames and Hudson, 1988.

Bürger, Peter. *Theory of the Avant-Garde.* Trans. Michael Shaw. Minneapolis: U of Minnesota P, 1984.

Butterick, George F. *A Guide to* The Maximus Poems *of Charles Olson.* Berkeley: U of California P, 1978.

———. "The Mysterious Vision of Susan Howe." *North Dakota Quarterly* 55.4 (1987): 312–21.

Byrd, Don. *Charles Olson's* Maximus. Urbana: U of Illinois P, 1980.

Cage, John. *Silence: Lectures and Writings by John Cage.* Middletown: Wesleyan UP, 1961.

———. *X: Writings '79–'82.* Middletown: Wesleyan UP, 1983.

Calinescu, Matei. *Five Faces of Modernity.* Durham: Duke UP, 1987.

Chamberlain, Lori. "Ghostwriting the Text: Translation and the Poetics of Jack Spicer." *Contemporary Literature* 26.4 (1985): 426–42.

Clark, Tom. *Charles Olson: The Allegory of a Poet's Life.* New York: Norton, 1991.

Clay, Steven, and Rodney Phillips. *A Secret Location on the Lower East Side: Adventures in Writing, 1960–1980.* New York: New York Public Library and Granary Books, 1998.

*Common Ground* 1.1 (1940). Statement of purpose on inside front cover.

Conte, Joseph M. *Unending Design: The Forms of Postmodern Poetry.* Ithaca: Cornell UP, 1991.

Damon, Maria. *The Dark End of the Street: Margins in American Vanguard Poetry.* Minneapolis: U of Minnesota P, 1993.

Davidson, Michael. *Ghostlier Demarcations: Modern Poetry and the Material Word.* Berkeley: U of California P, 1997.

———. *The San Francisco Renaissance: Poetics and Community at Mid-century.* Cambridge: Cambridge UP, 1989.

Delville, Michel. *The American Prose Poem: Poetic Form and the Boundaries of Genre.* Gainesville: UP of Florida, 1998.

Dent, Tom. "Lorenzo Thomas." *Afro-American Poets since 1955.* Vol. 41 of *Dictionary of Literary Biography.* Detroit: Gale, 1985. 315–26.

Doria, Charles. "Pound, Olson, and the Classical Tradition." *Boundary 2* 2.1–2 (1973–74): 127–43.

Drucker, Johanna. *The Century of Artists' Books.* New York: Granary, 1995.

———. *Figuring the Word: Essays on Books, Writing, and Visual Poetics.* New York: Granary, 1998.

———. *The History of the/my Wor(l)d.* 1990. New York: Granary, 1995.

———. *Simulant Portrait.* Riverdale, MD: Pyramid Atlantic, 1990.

———. *The Visible Word: Experimental Typography and Modern Art, 1909–1923.* Chicago: U of Chicago P, 1994.

Duncan, Robert. *Bending the Bow.* New York: New Directions, 1968.

DuPlessis, Rachel Blau. *The Pink Guitar: Writing as Feminist Practice.* New York: Routledge, 1990.

Dworkin, Craig Douglas. "'Waging Political Babble': Susan Howe's Visual Prosody and the Politics of Noise." *Word & Image* 12.4 (1996): 389–405.

Eisenhower, Dwight D. "Art of Peace." Address before the General Assembly of the United Nations, 1953. *Peace with Justice: Selected Addresses of Dwight D. Eisenhower.* New York: Columbia UP, 1961. 54–65.

———. Inaugural Address, 1953. *Peace with Justice: Selected Addresses of Dwight D. Eisenhower.* New York: Columbia UP, 1961. 25–33.

Ellingham, Lewis, and Kevin Killian. *Poet Be Like God: Jack Spicer and the San Francisco Renaissance.* Hanover: UP of New England, 1998.

Ellison, Ralph. *Invisible Man.* New York: Random, 1952.

Emerson, Ralph Waldo. *The Complete Writings of Ralph Waldo Emerson.* Vol. 1. New York: Wise, 1929.

Eshleman, Clayton. "The Lorca Working." *Boundary 2* 6.1 (1977): 31–49.

Fawcett, Brian. "Agent of Language." Andrews and Bernstein 151–54.

Finkelstein, Norman. "Jack Spicer's Ghosts and the Gnosis of History." *Boundary 2* 9.2 (1981): 81–100.

Foster, Edward Halsey. *Jack Spicer.* Boise: Boise State U Western Writers Ser., 1991.

Fraser, Kathleen. "Line. On the Line. Lining up. Lined with. Between the Lines. Bottom Line." *The Line in Postmodern Poetry.* Ed. Robert Frank and Henry Sayre. Urbana: U of Illinois P, 1988. 152–74.

Fredman, Stephen. *The Grounding of American Poetry: Charles Olson and the Emersonian Tradition.* Cambridge: Cambridge UP, 1993.

———. *Poet's Prose: The Crisis in American Verse.* 2nd ed. Cambridge: Cambridge UP, 1990.

Fried, Michael. *Absorption and Theatricality: Painting and Beholder in the Age of Diderot.* Berkeley: U of California P, 1980.

Genette, Gérard. *Palimpsests: Literature in the Second Degree.* 1982. Trans. Channa Newman and Claude Doubinsky. Lincoln: U of Nebraska P, 1997.

———. *Paratexts: Thresholds of Interpretation.* 1987. Trans. Jane E. Lewin. Cambridge: Cambridge UP, 1997.

Gilbert, Sandra M., and Susan Gubar. *The Madwoman in the Attic: The Woman Writer and the Nineteenth-Century Literary Imagination*. New Haven: Yale UP, 1979.

Gioia, Dana. *Can Poetry Matter?: Essays on Poetry and American Culture*. Saint Paul: Graywolf, 1992.

Gizzi, Peter. "Jack Spicer and the Practice of Reading." Spicer, *House* 173–225.

Golding, Alan. *From Outlaw to Classic: Canons in American Poetry*. Madison: U of Wisconsin P, 1995.

Granger, John. From "The Idea of the Alien." *Ironwood* 28 (1986): 165–86.

Greer, Michael. "Ideology and Theory in Recent Experimental Writing or, the Naming of 'Language Poetry.'" *Boundary 2* 16.2–3 (1989): 335–55.

Gropius, Walter. "Bauhaus Program." Trans. Hans M. Wingler. Long 247–49.

Hartley, George. *Textual Politics and the Language Poets*. Bloomington: Indiana UP, 1989.

Hartley, Marsden. *On Art*. Ed. Gail R. Scott. New York: Horizon, 1982.

Hassan, Ihab. *The Postmodern Turn: Essays in Postmodern Theory and Culture*. Columbus: Ohio State UP, 1987.

Hatlen, Burton. "Crawling into Bed with Sorrow: Jack Spicer's *After Lorca*." *Ironwood* 28 (1986): 118–35.

H.D. *Collected Poems 1912–1944*. Ed. Louis Martz. New York: New Directions, 1983.

Hogue, Cynthia. "Infectious Ecstasy: Toward a Poetics of Performative Transformation." *Women Poets of the Americas: Toward a Pan-American Gathering*. Ed. Jacqueline Vaught Brogan and Cordelia Chávez Candelaria. Notre Dame: U of Notre Dame P, 1999. 51–67.

Hokanson, Robert O'Brien. "'Projecting' like a Man: Charles Olson and the Poetics of Gender." *Sagetrieb* 9.1–2 (1990): 169–83.

Howard, W. Scott. "'Writing Ghost Writing': A Discursive Poetics of History; or Howe's 'Hau' in Susan Howe's 'A Bibliography of the King's Book; or, Eikon Basilike.'" *Talisman* 14 (1995): 108–30.

Howe, Susan. *The Birth-mark: Unsettling the Wilderness in American Literary History*. Hanover: UP of New England, 1993.

———. *The Europe of Trusts*. Los Angeles: Sun & Moon, 1990.

———. Interview with Janet Ruth Falon. 1986. *The Difficulties* 3.2 (1989): 28–42.

———. Interview with Tom Beckett. *The Difficulties* 3.2 (1989): 17–27.

———. *My Emily Dickinson*. Berkeley: North Atlantic, 1985.

———. *The Nonconformist's Memorial: Poems by Susan Howe*. New York: New Directions, 1993.

———. *Singularities*. Hanover: UP of New England, 1990.

———. "Where Should the Commander Be." *Writing* 19 (1987): 3–20.

Hubert, Renée Riese, and Judd D. Hubert. *The Cutting Edge of Reading: Artists' Books.* New York: Granary, 1999.

Huelsenbeck, Richard. "En Avant Dada: A History of Dadaism." Trans. Ralph Manheim. Motherwell 23–47.

Hutchinson, George. "The Pleistocene in the Projective: Some of Olson's Origins." *American Literature* 54.1 (1982): 81–96.

Jonas, Stephen. *Selected Poems.* Ed. Joseph Torra. Hoboken: Talisman, 1994.

Kalaidjian, Walter. "Transpersonal Poetics: Language Writing and the Historical Avant-Gardes in Postmodern Culture." *American Literary History* 3.2 (1991): 319–36.

Keller, Lynn. *Forms of Expansion: Recent Long Poems by Women.* Chicago: U of Chicago P, 1997.

Kellogg, David. "Body Poetics, Body Politics: The Birth of Charles Olson's Dynamic." *Sagetrieb* 10.3 (1991): 63–82.

Kostelanetz, Richard. *Dictionary of the Avant-Gardes.* Pennington, NJ: A Cappella, 1993.

Krauss, Rosalind E. *The Originality of the Avant-Garde and Other Modernist Myths.* Cambridge: MIT P, 1985.

Kuberski, Philip. "Charles Olson and the American Thing: The Ideology of Literary Revolution." *Criticism* 27.2 (1985): 175–93.

Larionov, Mikhail, and Natalya Goncharova. "Rayonists and Futurists: A Manifesto." Bowlt 87–91.

Lazer, Hank. *Opposing Poetries I: Issues and Institutions.* Evanston: Northwestern UP, 1996.

Lewis, Wyndham. Manifesto. BLAST 1. 1914. Santa Barbara: Black Sparrow, 1981: 9–43.

Long, Rose-Carol Washton, ed. *German Expressionism: Documents from the End of the Wilhelmine Empire to the Rise of National Socialism.* New York: Hall, 1993.

Lorca, Federico García. *The Selected Poems of Federico García Lorca.* New York: New Directions, 1955.

Lowney, John. *The American Avant-Garde Tradition: William Carlos Williams, Postmodern Poetry, and the Politics of Cultural Memory.* Lewisburg: Bucknell UP, 1997.

Ma, Ming-Qian. "Articulating the Inarticulate: Singularities and the Counter-Method in Susan Howe." *Contemporary Literature* 36.3 (1995): 466–89.

———. "Poetry as History Revised: Susan Howe's 'Scattering As Behavior Toward Risk.'" *American Literary History* 6.4 (1994): 716–37.

Malevich, Kazimir. *From Cubism and Futurism to Suprematism: The New Painterly Realism.* Bowlt 116–35.

Mann, Paul. *The Theory-Death of the Avant-Garde.* Bloomington: Indiana UP, 1991.

Marinetti, Filippo Tommaso. *Let's Murder the Moonshine: Selected Writings.* Ed. R. W. Flint. Los Angeles: Sun & Moon, 1991.

Marsh, Nicky. "'Out of My Texts I Am Not What I Play': Politics and Self in the Poetry of Susan Howe." *College Literature* 24.3 (1997): 124–37.

Matthiessen, F. O. Commentary in Pound symposium. *PM.* Sunday November 25, 1945: m16–m17.

Mayer, Bernadette. "Experiments." Andrews and Bernstein 80–83.

McCaffery, Steve. *North of Intention: Critical Writings 1973–1986.* New York: Roof, 1986.

McCarthy, Joseph R. "Communists in the State Department." Speech at Wheeling, West Virginia, February 1950. *The Annals of America* 17 (1950–60); Chicago: Benton, 1968. 16–21.

———. "A Conspiracy of Blackest Infamy." Speech on June 14, 1951. *The Fear of Conspiracy.* Ed. David Brion Davis. Ithaca: Cornell UP, 1971, 304–9.

McGann, Jerome J. "Contemporary Poetry, Alternate Routes." von Hallberg, *Politics* 253–76.

Meidner, Ludwig. "An Introduction to Painting the Metropolis." Trans. Victor H. Meisel. Long 101–4.

Melnick, David. *Men in Aida, Book One.* Berkeley: Tuumba, 1983.

Melville, Herman. *Billy Budd, Sailor (An Inside Narrative): Reading Text and Genetic Text.* Ed. Harrison Hayford and Merton M. Sealts Jr. Chicago: U of Chicago P, 1962.

Motherwell, Robert, ed. *The Dada Painters and Poets: An Anthology.* 2nd ed. Cambridge, MA: Belknap, 1981.

Murphy, Richard. *Theorizing the Avant-Garde: Modernism, Expressionism, and the Problem of Postmodernity.* Cambridge: Cambridge UP, 1999.

Nathanson, Tenney. "Collage and Pulverization in Contemporary American Poetry: Charles Bernstein's *Controlling Interests.*" *Contemporary Literature* 33.2 (1992): 302–18.

Naylor, Paul. "(Mis)Characterizing Charlie: Language and the Self in the Poetry and Poetics of Charles Bernstein." *Sagetrieb* 14.3 (1995): 119–38.

Nicholls, Peter. "Unsettling the Wilderness: Susan Howe and American History." *Contemporary Literature* 37.4 (1996): 586–601.

Nielsen, Aldon Lynn. *Black Chant: Languages of African-American Postmodernism.* Cambridge: Cambridge UP, 1997.

Olson, Charles. *Charles Olson and Robert Creeley: The Complete Correspondence.* Ed. Richard Blevins. Vol. 9. Santa Rosa: Black Sparrow, 1990.

————. *Charles Olson in Mansfield: Last Lectures.* Transcribed by John Cech, Oliver Ford, and Peter Rittner. Boston: Northeastern UP: 1977.

————. *The Collected Poems of Charles Olson, Excluding the* Maximus *Poems.* Ed. George F. Butterick. Berkeley: U of California P, 1987.

————. *Collected Prose.* Ed. Donald Allen and Benjamin Friedlander. Berkeley: U of California P, 1997.

————. *Letters for* Origin *1950–1956.* 1969. Ed. Albert Glover. New York: Paragon, 1989.

————. *The Maximus Poems.* Ed. George F. Butterick. Berkeley: U of California P, 1983.

————. *Mayan Letters.* Ed. Robert Creeley. Mallorca: Divers, 1953.

————. *Muthologos: The Collected Lectures and Interviews.* Ed. George F. Butterick. 2 vols. Bolinas: Four Seasons Foundation, 1978–79.

————. *Pleistocene Man: Letters from Charles Olson to John Clarke During October 1965.* Buffalo: The Institute of Further Studies, 1968.

————. *The Special View of History.* Ed. Ann Charters. Berkeley: Oyez, 1970.

Palattella, John. "An End of Abstraction: An Essay on Susan Howe's Historicism." *Denver Quarterly* 29.3 (1995): 74–97.

Perelman, Bob. *The Marginalization of Poetry: Language Writing and Literary History.* Princeton: Princeton UP, 1996.

————. *The Trouble with Genius: Reading Pound, Joyce, Stein, and Zukofsky.* Berkeley: U of California P, 1994.

Perloff, Marjorie. *The Dance of the Intellect: Studies in the Poetry of the Pound Tradition.* Cambridge: Cambridge UP, 1985.

————. "Essaying: Hot and Cool." *Michigan Quarterly Review* 26.2 (1987): 404–12.

————. *The Futurist Moment: Avant-Garde, Avant Guerre, and the Language of Rupture.* Chicago: U of Chicago P, 1986.

————. "Johanna Drucker's Herstory." *Harvard Library Bulletin* 3.2 (1992): 54–63.

————. *Poetic License: Essays on Modernist and Postmodernist Lyric.* Evanston: Northwestern UP, 1990.

Poggioli, Renato. *The Theory of the Avant-Garde.* Trans. Gerald Fitzgerald. Cambridge, MA: Belknap, 1968.

Pound, Ezra. *"Ezra Pound Speaking": Radio Speeches of World War II.* Ed. Leonard W. Doob. Westport: Greenwood, 1978.

————. *Literary Essays of Ezra Pound.* Ed. T. S. Eliot. London: Faber, 1954.

————. *Selected Prose: 1909–1965.* Ed. William Cookson. New York: New Directions, 1973.

———. "VORTEX. POUND." *BLAST* 1. 1914. Santa Barbara: Black Sparrow, 1981. 153–54.

Quartermain, Peter. *Disjunctive Poetics: From Gertrude Stein and Louis Zukofsky to Susan Howe.* Cambridge: Cambridge UP, 1992.

Rasula, Jed. "The Politics of, the Politics In." von Hallberg, *Politics* 315–22.

Reinfeld, Linda. *Language Poetry: Writing as Rescue.* Baton Rouge: Louisiana State UP, 1992.

Rich, Adrienne. *Adrienne Rich's Poetry and Prose.* Ed. Barbara Charlesworth Gelpi and Albert Gelpi. New York: Norton, 1993.

Riddel, Joseph. *The Inverted Bell: Modernism and the Counterpoetics of William Carlos Williams.* 1974. Baton Rouge: Louisiana State UP, 1991.

Sauer, Carl Ortwin. *Land and Life: A Selection from the Writings of Carl Ortwin Sauer.* Ed. John Leighly. Berkeley: U of California P, 1963.

Schmidt, Paul Ferdinand. "The Expressionists." Long 13–15.

Schultz, Susan M. "Visions of Silence in Poems of Ann Lauterbach and Charles Bernstein." *Talisman* 13 (1994–95): 163–77.

Sherry, James. "A,B,$." Andrews and Bernstein 165–67.

Shetley, Vernon. *After the Death of Poetry: Poet and Audience in Contemporary America.* Durham: Duke UP, 1993.

Silliman, Ron. "Disappearance of the Word, Appearance of the World." Andrews and Bernstein 121–32.

Spicer, Jack. *The Collected Books of Jack Spicer.* Ed. Robin Blaser. Santa Rosa: Black Sparrow, 1975.

———. *The House That Jack Built: The Collected Lectures of Jack Spicer.* Ed. Peter Gizzi. Hanover: UP of New England, 1998.

———. "Letters to Robin Blaser, 1955–58." Transcribed by Lori Chamberlain. *Line: A Journal of Contemporary Writing and Its Modernist Sources* 9 (1987): 26–55.

———. *One Night Stand & Other Poems.* Ed. Donald Allen. San Francisco: Grey Fox, 1980.

Stein, Gertrude. *Selected Writings.* 1962. Ed. Carl van Vechten. New York: Vintage, 1990.

Thomas, Lorenzo. *The Bathers.* New York: I. Reed, 1981.

———. "'Between the Comedy of Matters and the Ritual Workings of Man': An Interview with Lorenzo Thomas." With Charles H. Rowell. *Callaloo: A Journal of African-American Arts and Letters.* 4.1–3 (1981): 19–35.

———. *Chances are Few.* Berkeley: Blue Wind, 1979.

Tzara, Tristan. "Seven Dada Manifestoes." Trans. Ralph Manheim. Motherwell 73–98.

Vanderborg, Susan. "'If This Were the Place to Begin': Little Magazines and the Early Language Poetry Scene." *The World in Time and Space*. Ed. Edward Foster. Hoboken: Talisman, 2001.

Venuti, Lawrence. *The Translator's Invisibility: A History of Translation*. London: Routledge, 1995.

von Hallberg, Robert. *American Poetry and Culture, 1945–1980*. Cambridge: Harvard UP, 1985.

———. *Charles Olson: The Scholar's Art*. Cambridge: Harvard UP, 1978.

———, ed. *Politics & Poetic Value*. Chicago: U of Chicago P, 1987.

Waldrop, Rosmarie. *A Key into the Language of America*. New York: New Directions, 1994.

———. *The Reproduction of Profiles*. New York: New Directions, 1987.

Watten, Barrett. "Robert Grenier, *Sentences*." Andrews and Bernstein 235–37.

Williams, Megan. "Howe Not to Erase(her): A Poetics of Posterity in Susan Howe's *Melville's Marginalia*." *Contemporary Literature* 38.1 (1997): 106–32.

Williams, William Carlos. Comment. *Contact* 2 (1921): 11–12. New York: Kraus Reprint Corp., 1967.

———. *Kora in Hell: Improvisations*. *Imaginations*. New York: New Directions, 1970. 6–82.

Zdanevich, Ilya, and Mikhail Larionov. "Why We Paint Ourselves: A Futurist Manifesto." Bowlt 79–83.

# Index

*Susan Vanderborg* is an assistant professor at the University of South Carolina, Columbia, in the field of twentieth-century American experimental poetry. Her publications include articles on the poetry of Louis Zukofsky, Charles Olson, and Susan Howe, as well as on small press poetry magazines of the seventies and eighties.